GREAT 100 IDEAS
FOR
KITCHEN CENTERS

ANNETTE DePAEPE CKD, CBD, ASID

Edited by Stacy Michaelson

Drawings by Annette DePaepe, CKD, CBD, ASID

Miller Freeman Books
San Francisco

100 Great Ideas For Kitchen Centers

 Published by Miller Freeman Books
600 Harrison Street
San Francisco, CA 94107
Publishers of KBB Kitchen & Bath Business
magazine
A member of United News & Media Group

Book and cover design: Nina Clayton
Cover illustrations: Annette DePaepe CKD, CBD, ASID

ISBN 0-87930-537-1

Printed in the United States of America
98 99 01 02 03   5 4 3 2 1

Table of Contents

About the Author

Annette M. DePaepe, CKD, CBD, ASID, **holds a Bachelor of Fine Arts degree in interior design and space planning and is NCIDQ certified.**

In her 15 years of industry experience, she has worked as an independent designer, retail showroom consultant and graphic illustrator. She has also administrated NKBA certification programs and been involved in special projects management.

Currently Annette is president of AMD Designs in Hackettstown, N.J., specializing in the design of kitchen/bathroom/furniture showrooms and exhibit displays for the trade, as well as interior illustration and publishing/research services. She has both won and judged national design competitions, has had numerous designs published in national consumer magazines, and has authored and illustrated a number of industry-related textbooks. This is her third in a series of design idea books published in conjunction with *Kitchen & Bath Business* magazine.

Acknowledgments

The completion of this book would not have been possible without the contribution of several individuals.

In 1992 Nick Geragi, CKD, CBD, ASID, wrote a series of articles for KBB called "Kitchen Ideas Notebook." Back then, he had a vision that these articles had the makings of a series of design idea books and now, as I complete this third book, I believe his vision has materialized. I remain very honored that he entrusted me to fulfill the vision. Thank you, my husband, for sharing, trusting and supporting me in this, just as you do in every other aspect of our lives together.

A very special and personal thank you to B. Leslie Hart, the publisher and editorial director of KBB, who stuck her neck out professionally and took a chance on an unknown. Then, she did it again and again. First, it was *100 Great Ideas for Islands*, then *100+ Great Ideas for Moldings* and now *100 Great Ideas for Kitchen Centers*. Leslie, you have not only made the original vision a reality, but you have also helped me to realize my own abilities.

Thanks to Stacy Michaelson, managing editor of KBB, for making sense out of everything I write. Stacy is responsible for editing every sentence and handling the book's overall production. Thank you for attempting to keep me on schedule and never making me feel guilty for missing a deadline.

Credit for the cover design, as well as the overall design and layout of the book, goes to Nina Clayton. Thank you Nina, for making the book seem to flow effortlessly from page to page and chapter to chapter.

I would also like to thank Sarah Reep, CKD, ASID, Director of Design and Education at Fieldstone Cabinetry, for freely sharing her ideas, designs and industry contacts to help make this book, as well as *100+ Great Ideas for Moldings*, a success.

Finally, my thanks again to KBB for lending its name and unparalleled reputation as the industry's leading trade magazine for over 40 years. Our partnership continues to reward me in ways that I never imagined, and I look forward to future endeavors together.

Introduction

The emergence of new dynamics in contemporary households has brought tremendous change to the role of the kitchen, and thus, to our jobs as kitchen designers.

While in the past one person was generally in charge of the kitchen, with uses limited to food storage, meal preparation, serving and cleanup, today's kitchen space is used by every member of the household—often simultaneously and for a growing number of activities. These lifestyle changes, coupled with consumers' growing aesthetic preference for an unfitted look, mean that the most comfortable kitchen for your clients can often include five or more task-specific centers—a far more complicated design than the traditional work triangle.

Generally, kitchen centers can be divided into three categories; those designed for people to work at, those designed as storage facilities and the newest and ever-growing catchall category, those serving special and/or individual needs. The centers most frequented during meal preparation are cleanup, cooking and food storage (the traditional work triangle). New centers that often interrelate with this triangle include secondary cleanup and food preparation, baking, recycling, coffee/beverage or breakfast, serving, grilling, laundry, display, entertainment, home office, herb growing and other special needs or hobby centers.

A steady stream of innovative appliances, such as warming ovens, beverage chillers and point-of-use refrigeration, bring the designer greater opportunity to creatively meet the needs of today's diverse families and their lifestyles. A kitchen may have two or three triangles, it may form a triangle with various legs and/or intersections, or it may form another shape altogether, such as a rectangle or polygon.

Since a single kitchen center will likely serve diverse purposes and be used by different family members at various times of the day and week, universal design, once thought to be applicable only for the elderly or those using a wheelchair, should always be considered.

Using this book

In the practice of design, it is always a challenge to come up with new and interesting ideas that will meet the needs and wants of our customers. As design professionals we are committed to providing each and every client with personal attention and individual design advice. There are, however, a number of common elements that all kitchen designs inherently share. Perhaps the greatest of these are the appliances and other equipment that make up a kitchen's centers.

This book presents myriad kitchen center ideas, grouped by their functions into chapters. Each of the 100 projects presents both a perspective drawing and a floor plan. Unless otherwise stated, the plans are drawn to 1/2" scale. Some of the designs incorporate typical appliances and/or equipment uses, while others detail unusual situations and showcase special equipment and/or innovative cabinet uses. Some designs represent actual installations in homes around the world, and others are conceptual creations specifically generated for this publication.

Each designer whose concept is used in the book is credited on the page where his or her work appears. This is by no means intended to limit its use by you or your clients. On the

contrary, the designs should be used as a tool in your own design idea generation. I encourage you to photocopy pages from the book and use them in conceptual design presentations with your clients. If you and your client like an idea just the way it is presented, use it as it is and that part of your job is complete. It is more likely, however, that you will find one or two aspects of an idea that will work for your situation and these will serve as a springboard for new ideas.

The best and most successful solutions are often not original ideas unto themselves, but instead evolve from bits and pieces of previous solutions to previous challenges. It is how we choose to apply these ideas in our designs that is original. Perhaps we combine two old ideas in a new way, refine an old solution or alter an idea to meet the individuality of a new situation or client. That is how we, as design profes-

sionals, can best serve the homeowners who are our clients.

Planning Guidelines

As previously hinted at, the work triangle, while still the foundation for the design of the basic work/cook area, is no longer the golden rule of kitchen design. In fact, the National Kitchen & Bath Association has recently updated its message regarding kitchen planning by changing the old "planning rules" to new, unrestricted "planning guidelines."

Many of these guidelines, titled "40 Universal Guidelines for Kitchen Planning," directly affect the planning of kitchen work centers. Below, categorized by related kitchen center, are those that are applicable to the centers covered in this book. The guidelines provide fundamental adjacencies recommendations and minimum dimensions required to perform basic kitchen functions.

Cleanup Centers

There should be at least 24" of work counter on one side of the primary sink, and 18" on the other side (including corner sink applications), with the 24" work counter at the same height as the sink.

Allow for at least 3" of work counter on one side of a secondary sink, and 18" on the other side (including corner sink applications) with the 18" work counter at the same height as the sink.

At least two waste receptacles should be included in the kitchen. One for garbage and one for recyclables. (The recommended location is in or adjacent to a cleanup sink.)

A minimum of 21" of clear floor space should be provided between the edge of the dishwasher and counters/cabinets/appliances placed at a right angle to the dishwasher.

The edge of the dishwasher should be within 36" of the edge of a sink.

At least one sink should be located between or across from the cooking center, preparation center or refrigerator.

The preparation center should be immediately adjacent to a water source and should consist of at least 36" of continuous work counter.

Cooking Centers

The cooking surface should not be located below an operable window unless the window is 3" or more behind the appliance and more than 24" above it. Windows (operable or non-operable) should not be dressed with flammable window treatments.

In an open-ended kitchen configuration, at least 9" of work counter should be allowed on one side of the cooking surface and 15" on the other, at the same counter height of the appliances. For an enclosed configuration, at least 3" of clearance space should be planned at an end wall protected by a flame-retardant surfacing material, and 15" should be allowed on the other side of the appliance, at the same counter height of the appliance.

Microwave ovens should be placed so the bottom of the appliance is 24" to 48" above the floor.

At least 15" of landing space, a minimum of 16" deep, should be planned above, below or adjacent to the microwave.

There should be at least 15" of landing space at least 16" deep next to or above the oven if the door opens into a primary traffic pattern. If the oven does not open into a traffic area, at least 15" x 16" of landing space, located no more than 48" across from the oven, is acceptable.

Counter/Appliance Work Centers

At least two work-counter heights should be offered in the kitchen, with one 28" to 36" above the finished floor and the other 36" to 45" above the finished floor.

Work counters should be a minimum of 16" deep and wall cabinets should be at least 15" above the countertop surface.

Kneespace (open or adaptable) should be planned below or adjacent to sinks, cooktops, ranges, dishwashers, refrigerators and ovens whenever possible. They should be a minimum of 30" wide, 27" high and 19" deep.

A clear floor space of 30" x 48" should be provided in front of the sink, dishwasher, cooktop, oven and refrigerator.

No two primary work centers (cleanup/preparation, cook and refrigerator) should be separated by a full-height, full-depth tall tower such as an oven cabinet, pantry cabinet or refrigerator.

Controls, handles and door/drawer pulls should be operable with one hand and require only a minimum amount of strength for operation. They should not require tight grasping, pinching or twisting of the wrist.

Countertop corners should be clipped or radius; countertop edges should be eased to eliminate sharp edges.

A fire extinguisher should be visibly located in the kitchen, away from cooking equipment and 15" to 48" above the floor. Smoke alarms should be included in the kitchen.

Every work surface in the kitchen should be well illuminated by appropriate task and/or general light.

Food Storage Centers

The plan should allow at least 15" of work counter on the handle side of the refrigerator or on either side of a side-by-side refrigerator or at least 15" of landing space which is no more than 48" across from the refrigerator.

CHAPTER ONE

Sink Centers

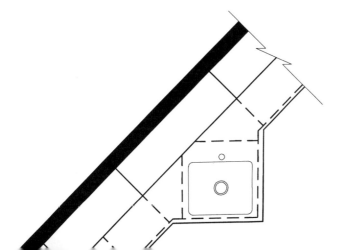

Designed **to resemble** freestanding furniture, this sink center would fit nicely into a 19th-century farmhouse. The base is supported at the front with three 4" x 4" balusters that terminate with ball-like feet. The left drawer box houses the sink and tilts out to hold sponges and other such items inside a stainless steel tray. A scalloped valance at the bottom of the drawer unit is repeated above in the open wall cabinet. The 30"-high x 66"-wide wall cabinet reduces from a standard 12" depth at the top to a 9" depth at the bottom. This both creates an interesting look and maximizes the work surface and sink area below. Beaded paneling on the backs of the wall and base cabinets adds traditional detail and helps tie the units together.

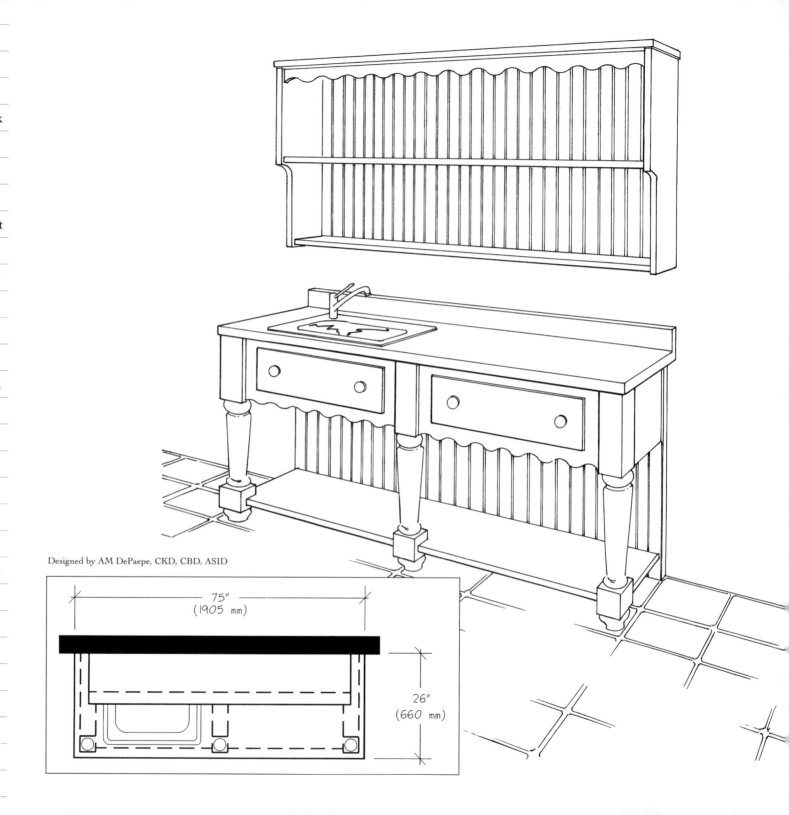

Designed by AM DePaepe, CKD, CBD, ASID

75"
(1905 mm)

26"
(660 mm)

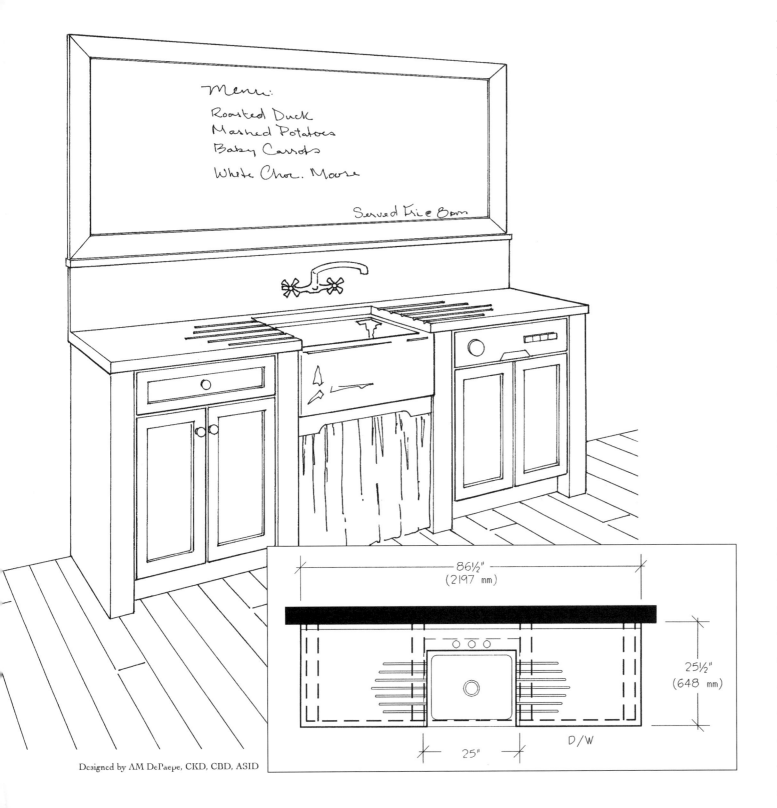

Menu:
Roasted Duck
Mashed Potatoes
Baby Carrots
White Choc. Moose

Served Fine 8pm

86½"
(2197 mm)

25½"
(648 mm)

25"

D/W

Designed by AM DePaepe, CKD, CBD, ASID

The functional elements of a restaurant kitchen combine with traditional ones to create this informal residential sink center. Its symmetrical design is anchored by a 25"-wide x 22"-deep undercounter sink with integral apron. A wall-mounted faucet and an arched valance with a fabric drape complete the look. A solid surface counter slopes slightly toward the center and incorporates a routed drainboard on either side of the sink; the sink is also flanked by a 24"-wide dishwasher and a 24"-wide base cabinet. These are sandwiched between 3"-wide filler return pilasters. Above the counter, a 12"-high backsplash protects the wall and supports a blackboard. The blackboard is framed with 3"-wide filler panels that are mitered at 45-degree angles.

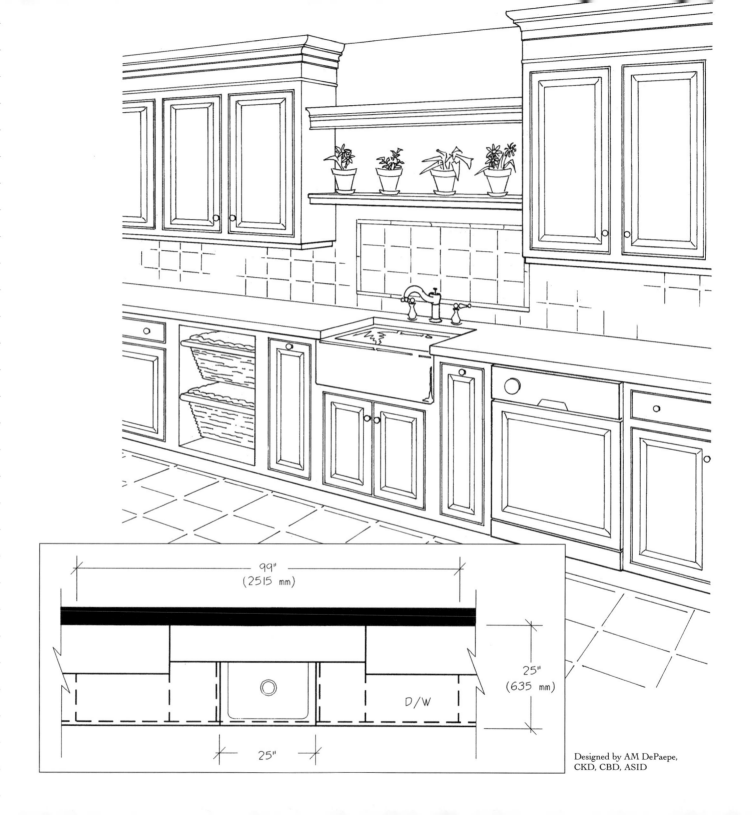

The fact that this sink center has no window doesn't detract from its pleasing view. A 51"-wide x 9"-deep valance and open shelf break the run of wall cabinets, creating an interior focal point above the sink. A mural framed with pencil strip tile adds emphasis. On either side of the sink, 36"-high wall cabinets with molding buildups extend to the 8' ceiling. Function is not forsaken for aesthetics, however: Task lighting for the sink is located under the shelf, and the 3"-high valance hides a growing lamp for potted herbs. The right side of the sink is designated for cleanup and storage, with a 12"-wide pullout base equipped with wire inserts. The left side of the sink is for food prep; its pullout base has rods for hanging dish towels and slots to store chopping boards.

99"
(2515 mm)

25"
(635 mm)

D/W

25"

Designed by AM DePaepe,
CKD, CBD, ASID

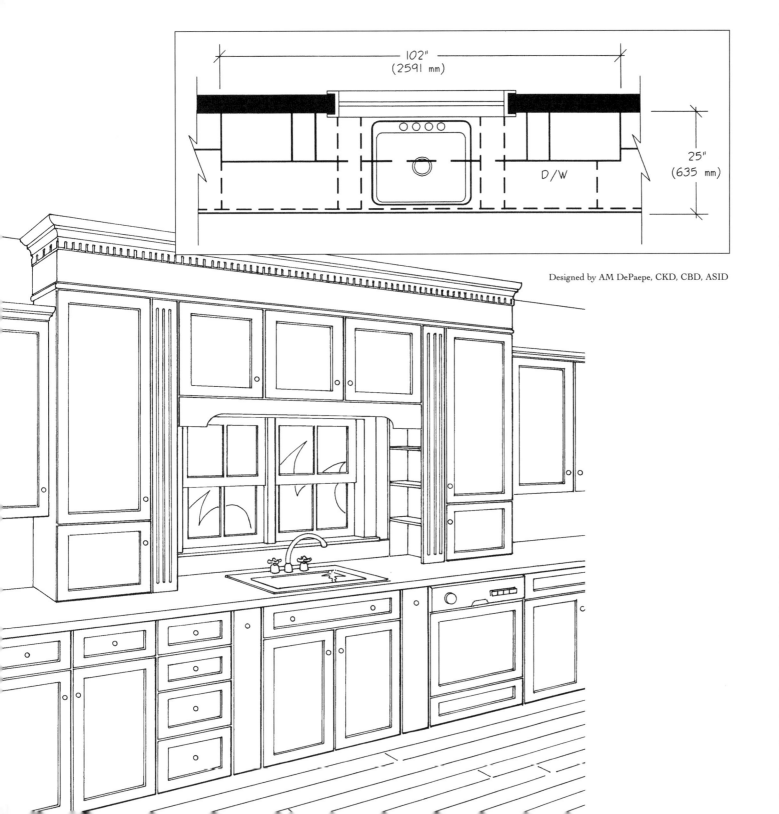

102"
(2591 mm)

25"
(635 mm)

D/W

Designed by AM DePaepe, CKD, CBD, ASID

Double-hung windows that measure 48" wide x 30" high from the outside of their casings are neatly framed with cabinets and moldings in this sink center. Three 18"-wide x 18"-high x 15"-deep cabinets and a 54"-wide x 6"-high arched valance start the frame. Fluted pillasters measuring 6" wide, 54" high and 15" deep house open shelves, keeping them hidden from most of the kitchen's view. Double-doored, 18"-wide, 54"-high, 15"-deep wall cabinets then extend down to the countertop. A facia, dentil and crown molding buildup tops the entire unit. Standard 30"-high x 12"-deep wall cabinets with small crown moldings wrap the remainder of the kitchen. Base cabinets include a 15"-wide drawer bank, two 6"-wide pullout units, a 30" sink base and a 24" dishwasher.

Three is the magic number in this sink center. Placed below three horizontal shelves, three casement windows sit above a triple bowl sink. A 93"-wide section of wall is pushed out 3", defining the primary work area. The windows measure 54" wide x 21" high from the outside of their casings. These shelves are supported by Arts & Crafts-style brackets that extend 9" deep. The window sill, which reaches out to the side wall cabinets, becomes another shelf. The sink sits in a 45"-wide base cabinet; a dishwasher and a three-drawer base unit sit on either side. Where the wall breaks, cabinets are extended to the counter. The side panels are extended to cover the adjacent wall area.

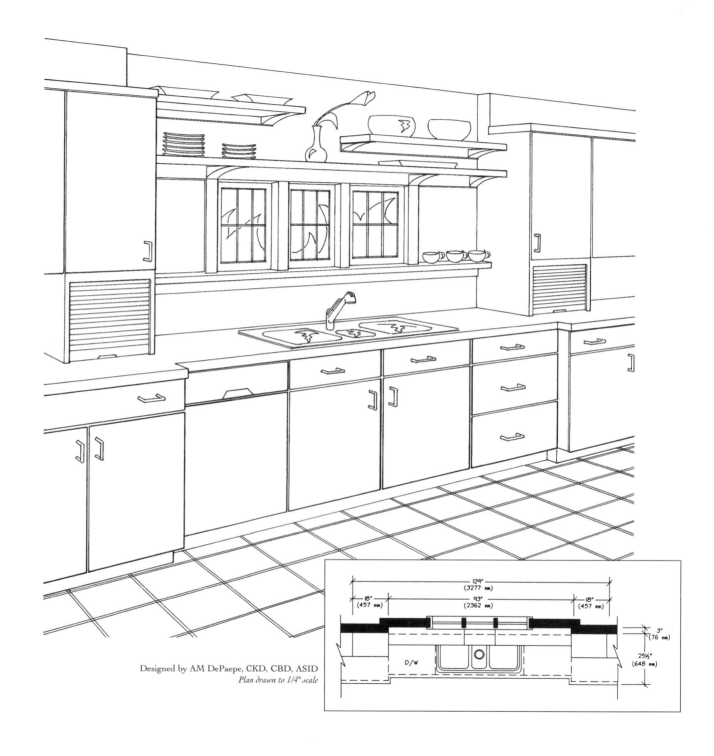

Designed by AM DePaepe, CKD, CBD, ASID
Plan drawn to 1/4" scale

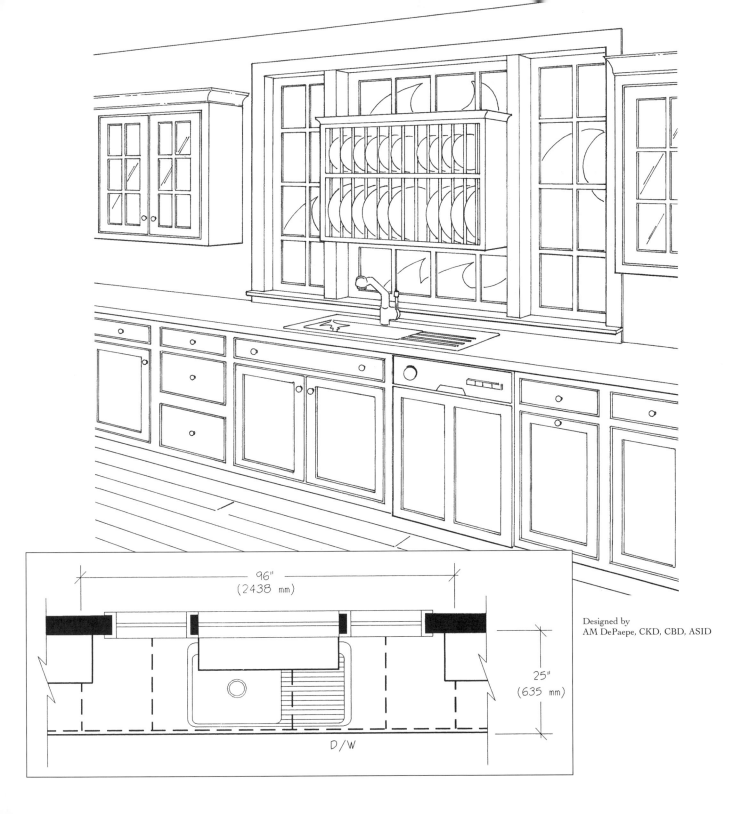

Designed by
AM DePaepe, CKD, CBD, ASID

While it is still desirable to include windows at a kitchen's primary sink area, homeowners rarely stand directly in front of the sink for long periods of time. This sink center offers major window views on either side of the sink while providing decorative open storage with a 36"-wide x 24"-high x 9"-deep plate rack. The window area, including the casings, is 84" wide x 54" high. The side windows operate as casements; the center ones can be fixed or operate as awnings. Below is a 36"-wide sink base and a 24"-wide dishwasher. An 18"-wide pullout waste basket with drawer above sits to the right of the dishwasher; an 18", three-drawer base is located to the left of the sink base. Wall cabinets with mullioned glass doors mimic the windows' look.

The curvilinear lines and forms of this sink center establish the kitchen's decorative motif. The double-bowl sink is set in a 36"-wide base that is pulled out 4" from the wall and adorned with an arched valance with a floral appliqué. The back panel is removable, providing access to plumbing. Pullout towel bar bases flank the sink cabinet. At 6"-wide, they are placed 30" deep, protruding 2" from the face of the sink base. Centered on the wall 9" above standard backsplash height is a 36"-wide, circle-top cabinet with mullioned glass doors. A valance with matching floral appliqué maintains the backsplash's horizontal line. Fluted 6"-wide x 12"-deep panels mirror the base units and provide space for the wall cabinets' crown molding to return with a mitered corner.

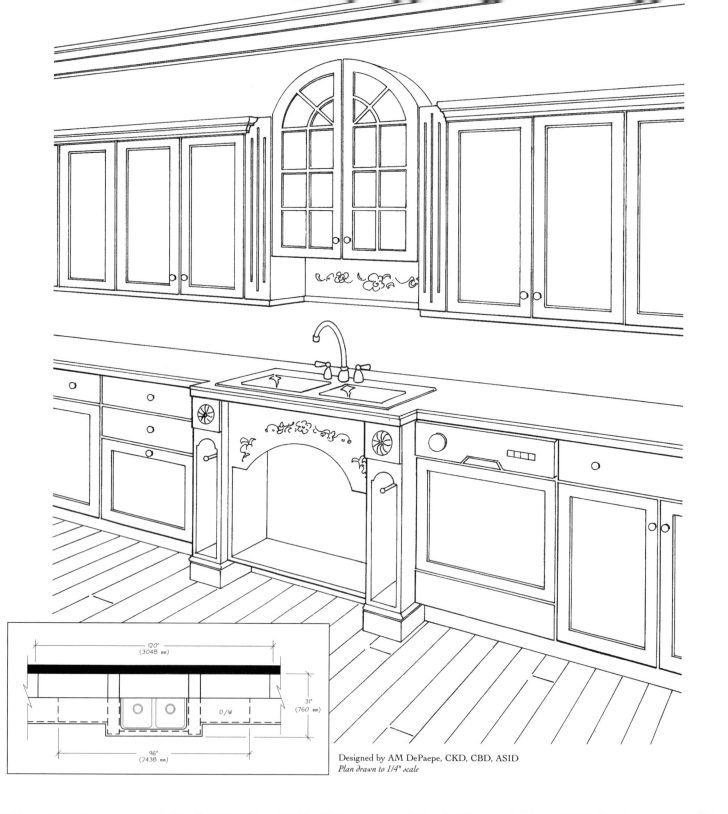

Designed by AM DePaepe, CKD, CBD, ASID
Plan drawn to 1/4" scale

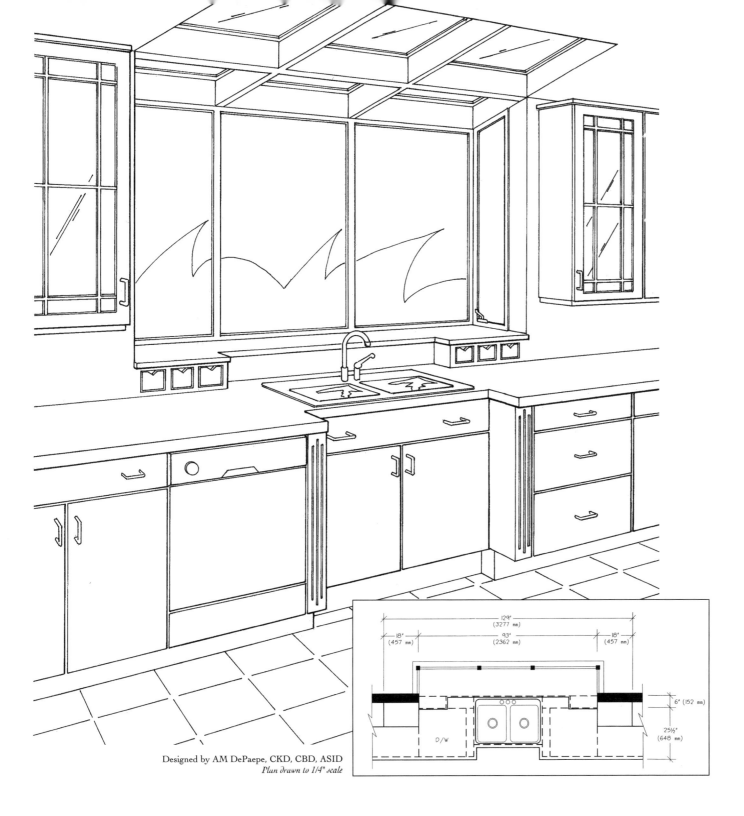

Designed by AM DePaepe, CKD, CBD, ASID
Plan drawn to 1/4" scale

Natural light floods this sink center from nearly every angle. A 93"-wide x 54"-high x 12"-deep garden window is combined with a grid of six skylights in the vaulted ceiling. The glass partially encloses the sink; the 36"-wide sink cabinet is recessed 6" into the window area, which is offset by a shelf/window ledge that steps back and to the sides another 6". The look is continued by the adjacent glass doors. The space just below the window ledge that is not stepped back contains three recessed apothecary drawers at each side—perfect for spice storage. The transition back to standard depth is made with 6" fluted fillers and returns on either side of the sink base. The center is completed with a 24"-wide dishwasher and a 24"-wide, three-drawer base cabinet.

To maximize countertop space, send the sink to the corner. This butterfly double-bowl sink uses only 30" of base cabinet frontage (15" in each direction) instead of the typical 36". Perched atop a 39"-wide corner base, the butterfly is captured from behind by a diagonal corner shelf. A dishwasher and 9" base with pullout storage help with cleanup; the extra 9" between the sink and the dishwasher allows for liberal space to load the dishwasher. An 18", three-drawer base and a 36" base to the right of the sink hold cooking supplies. Three 24"-wide x 27"-high wall cabinets with glass doors and 9"-high undercabinet shelves frame the corner. These align with the 36"-high wall cabinets and the continuous facia and crown molding, which run all the way up to the 8' ceiling.

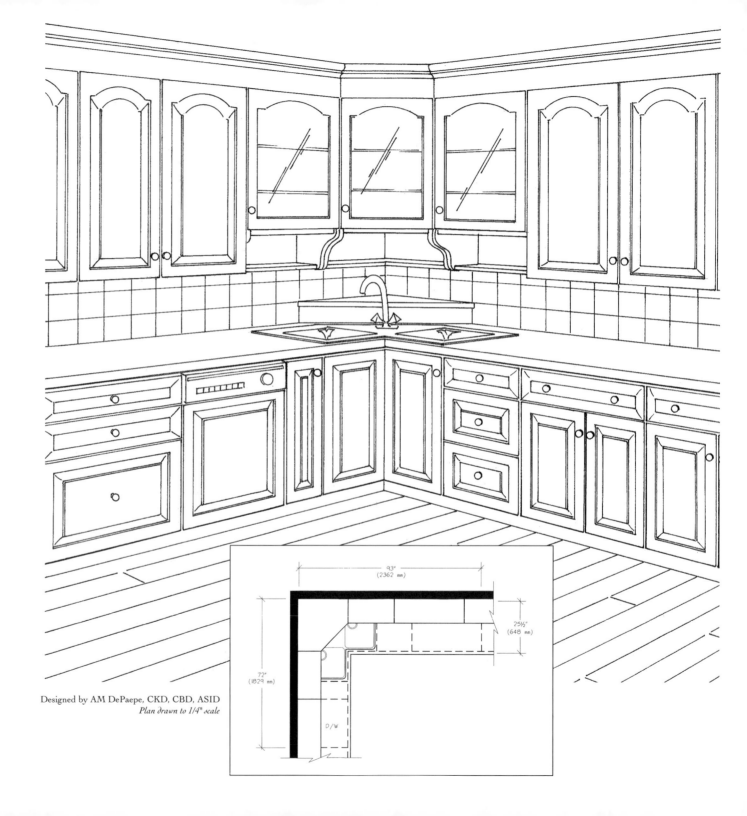

Designed by AM DePaepe, CKD, CBD, ASID
Plan drawn to 1/4" scale

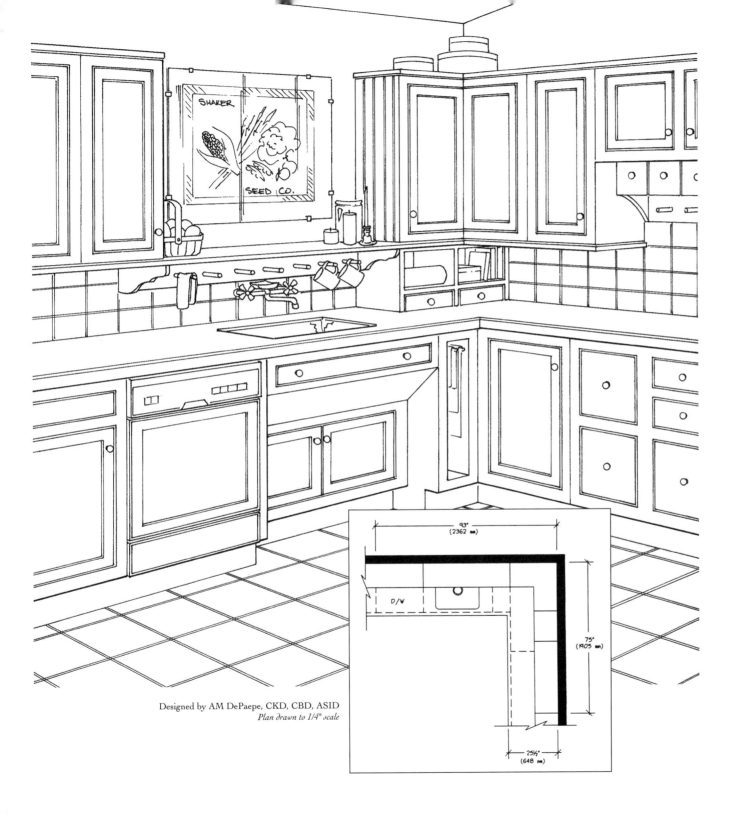

Designed by AM DePaepe, CKD, CBD, ASID
Plan drawn to 1/4" scale

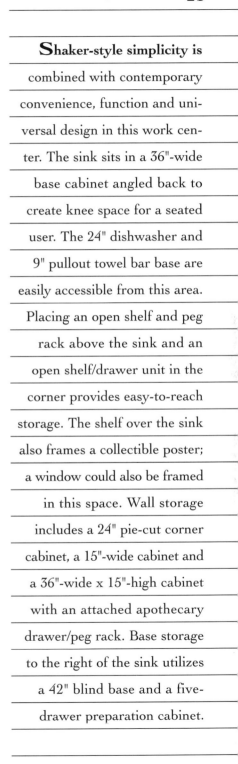

Shaker-style simplicity is combined with contemporary convenience, function and universal design in this work center. The sink sits in a 36"-wide base cabinet angled back to create knee space for a seated user. The 24" dishwasher and 9" pullout towel bar base are easily accessible from this area. Placing an open shelf and peg rack above the sink and an open shelf/drawer unit in the corner provides easy-to-reach storage. The shelf over the sink also frames a collectible poster; a window could also be framed in this space. Wall storage includes a 24" pie-cut corner cabinet, a 15"-wide cabinet and a 36"-wide x 15"-high cabinet with an attached apothecary drawer/peg rack. Base storage to the right of the sink utilizes a 42" blind base and a five-drawer preparation cabinet.

A small triangular peninsula equipped with an integral sink and a single-lever faucet with pullout spray lets two individuals access the sink at once. One user can rinse dishes and load the dishwasher to the left, while another prepares dessert to the right, using the spray to fill the coffee pot. The 24"-wide sink base is preceded by an 18" base, a 24" dishwasher, an 18", four-drawer base and a 6"-wide x 40 1/2"-high wine rack; the wine rack is topped with a 1 1/2"-high counter that wraps around to form a 6"-deep shelf along the back wall. The wall cabinets include a 42"-wide x 36"-high open shelf unit centered above the sink base. The angled area is highlighted by an extended soffit board with recessed lighting that follows the base cabinets' outline.

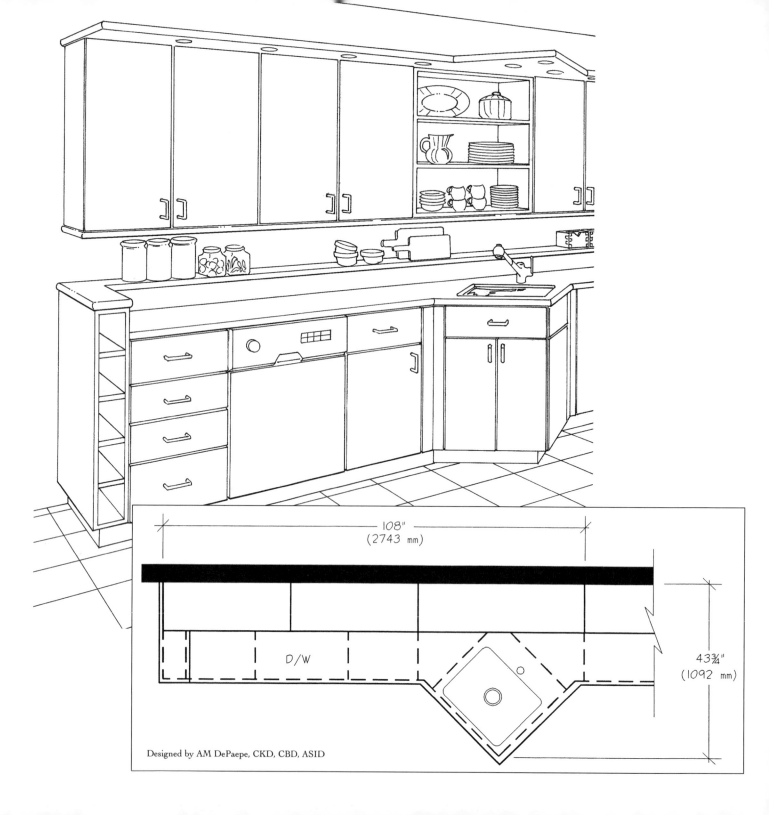

108"
(2743 mm)

43¾"
(1092 mm)

D/W

Designed by AM DePaepe, CKD, CBD, ASID

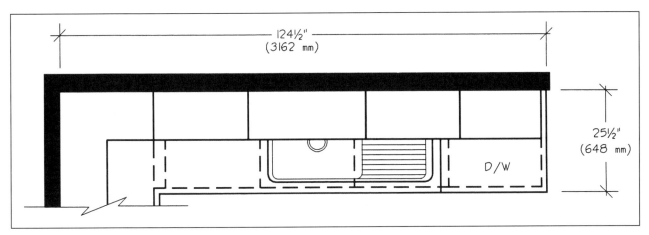

124½"
(3162 mm)

25½"
(648 mm)

D/W

Designed by AM DePaepe, CKD, CBD, ASID

Sleek and contemporary describe this convenience-minded design. Raising the dishwasher 16" above the floor by setting it atop a 12"-high drawer and a 4" toekick reduces the need to bend over. Finishing the tower are a 1 1/2"-high countertop and a 32"-high wall cabinet. A 24"-wide corner wall cabinet and a 24"-deep blind base cabinet define the left boundary of the work area. The base storage is made up of three 24"-wide cabinets. The wall cabinet bottoms are at 5' above the floor, allowing a high back-splash fitted with a rack. Above are two 24"-wide cabinets and a 30"-wide unit with one tilt-up door and one open shelf. An extended soffit board, a wrap countertop around the dish-washer and moldings with a curved profile complete the contemporary look.

Traditional charm and accessibility are the hallmarks of this sink work center. The farmhouse sink is left open to provide knee space for a seated user; the valance and fabric curtain retain its motif. Placing the sink diagonally underneath two windows makes the corner the focal point of the room. Raised counter space behind the sink forms a 5 1/2"-high splash guard and a triangular shelf. On either side of the sink are 12"-wide x 42"-high diagonal wall cabinets. To the right, a 36"-wide wall cabinet combines two 12"-high glass doors, two 15"-high doors and an open plate rack. To the left is a 21"-wide x 42"-high wall cabinet topped with 12"-high glass doors. Finishing details include recessed soffits extended to the 9' ceiling with crown molding.

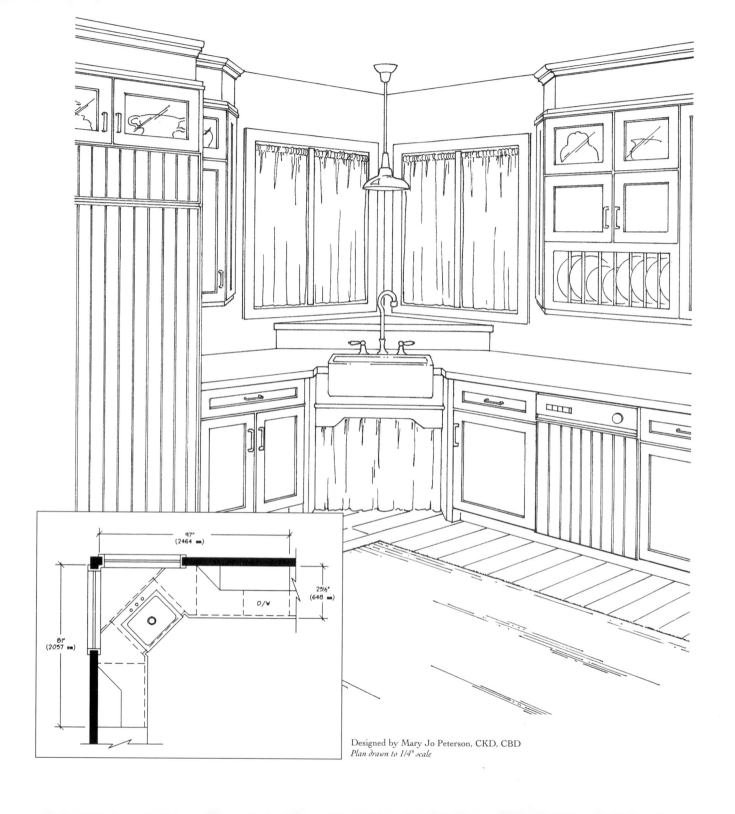

Designed by Mary Jo Peterson, CKD, CBD
Plan drawn to 1/4" scale

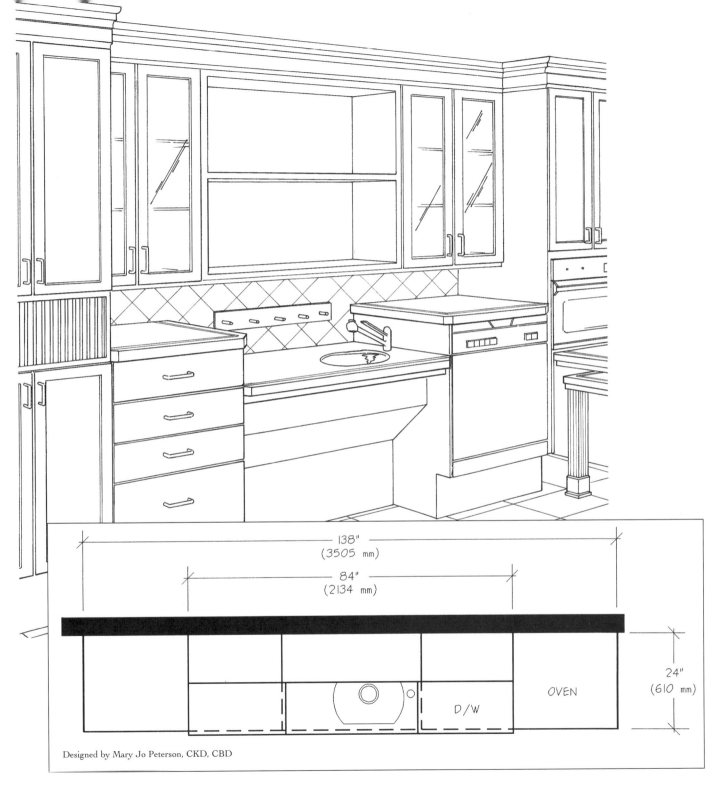

138"
(3505 mm)

84"
(2134 mm)

24"
(610 mm)

OVEN

D/W

Designed by Mary Jo Peterson, CKD, CBD

This 84"-long work center is designed to showcase universal design criteria including, but not limited to, wheelchair users. The sink counter area is lowered to 30" and includes a 36"-wide x 19"-deep knee space. Allowing for a wheelchair's footrest, the dishwasher, the 24", four-drawer base and one of the 27"-wide cabinets are raised on 12"-high toekicks. Two 24"-wide x 30"-high wall cabinets with glass doors sandwich the 36"-wide x 30"-high open shelf area above the sink. The two 27"-wide tall towers contain the cabinet run. The one on the left features an accessible open plate rack; the one on the right houses the microwave above a 30"-high pullout table. The table, left open to include knee space, provides a safe surface to rest hot foods.

This work center caters to the homeowner's desire for a convenient and attractive space. The integral bowl sink is set off center from the window to increase counter work surface on the right side. Integral drainboards on both sides of the sink and a wall-mounted faucet further maximize work space. The wall cabinets are encased in 24"-wide arched niches that span from the countertops to the ceiling. The niche on the right encloses a glass-doored cabinet with a drawer on the bottom. The one on the left is open and fitted with five shelves. The base cabinets include a 15"-wide base unit, a 36"-wide sink base, a dishwasher and a wine cooler. The counter surface is dropped at the left corner to create a 30"-high baking counter with 28 1/2"-high bases underneath.

Designed by Kathleen Donohue, CKD, CBD
Plan drawn to 1/4" scale

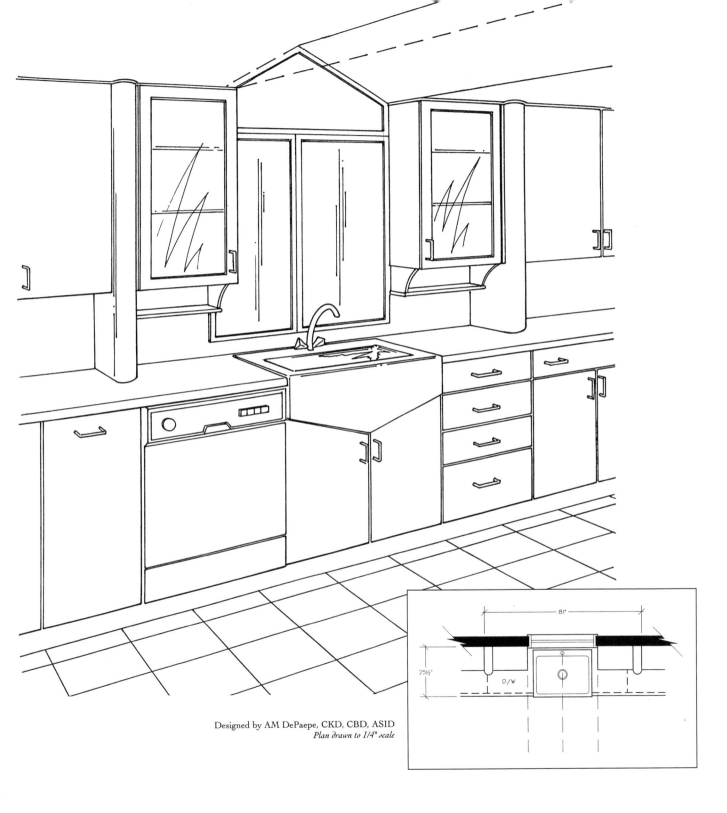

Designed by AM DePaepe, CKD, CBD, ASID
Plan drawn to 1/4" scale

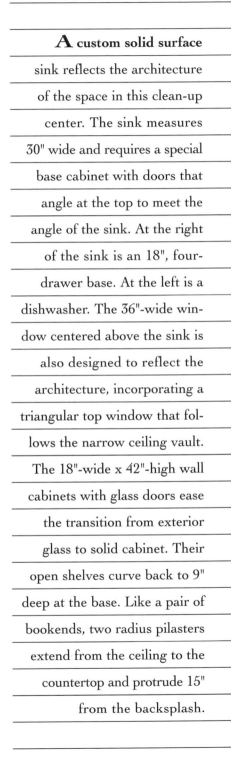

A **custom solid surface** sink reflects the architecture of the space in this clean-up center. The sink measures 30" wide and requires a special base cabinet with doors that angle at the top to meet the angle of the sink. At the right of the sink is an 18", four-drawer base. At the left is a dishwasher. The 36"-wide window centered above the sink is also designed to reflect the architecture, incorporating a triangular top window that follows the narrow ceiling vault. The 18"-wide x 42"-high wall cabinets with glass doors ease the transition from exterior glass to solid cabinet. Their open shelves curve back to 9" deep at the base. Like a pair of bookends, two radius pilasters extend from the ceiling to the countertop and protrude 15" from the backsplash.

CHAPTER TWO

Cooking Centers

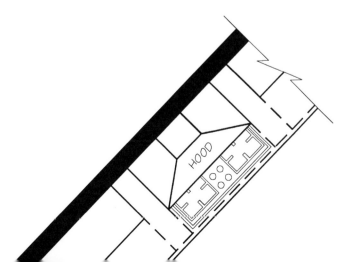

Contemporary country style provides fingertip convenience at this work station. The professional cooktop is set in a 36"-wide x 26 1/2"-high x 27"-deep cabinet. Open-faced base cabinets on either side of the cooktop hold utensils and fresh foods. These 18"-wide cabinets are pulled away from the wall 3" to match the 27" depth of the cooktop base. Each cabinet features two pull-out drawers and two pullout baskets. Keeping the wall cabinets outside the 72" cooking area makes the stainless hood and cantilevered shelf the focal point of the room. The shelf is held 12" below the top of the adjacent wall cabinets and 72" above the floor. The remaining wall area is filled with a spice rack, a blackboard and a utensil rack, which is mounted below the hood.

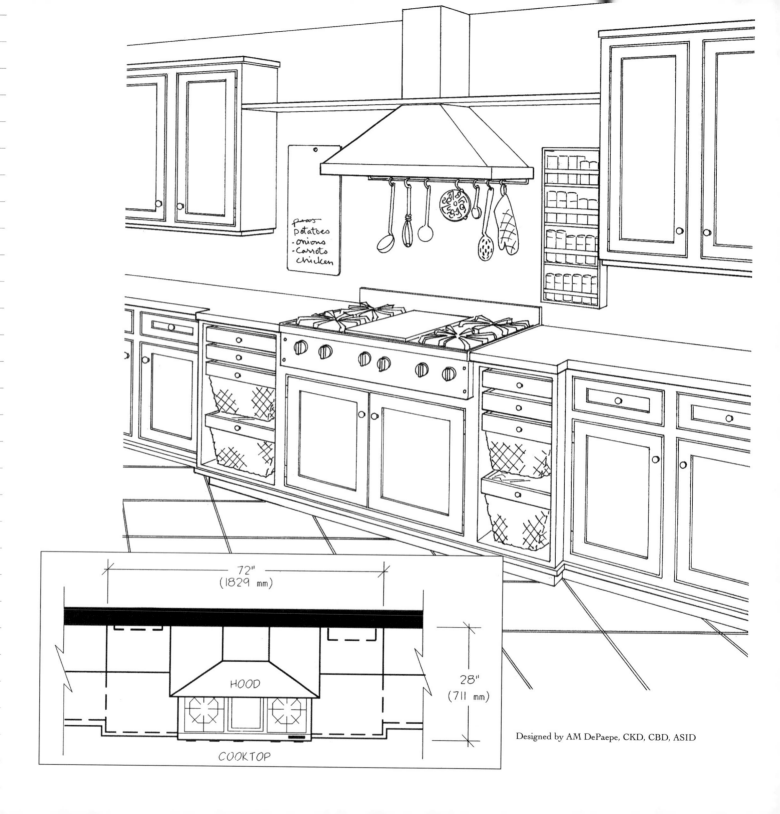

Designed by AM DePaepe, CKD, CBD, ASID

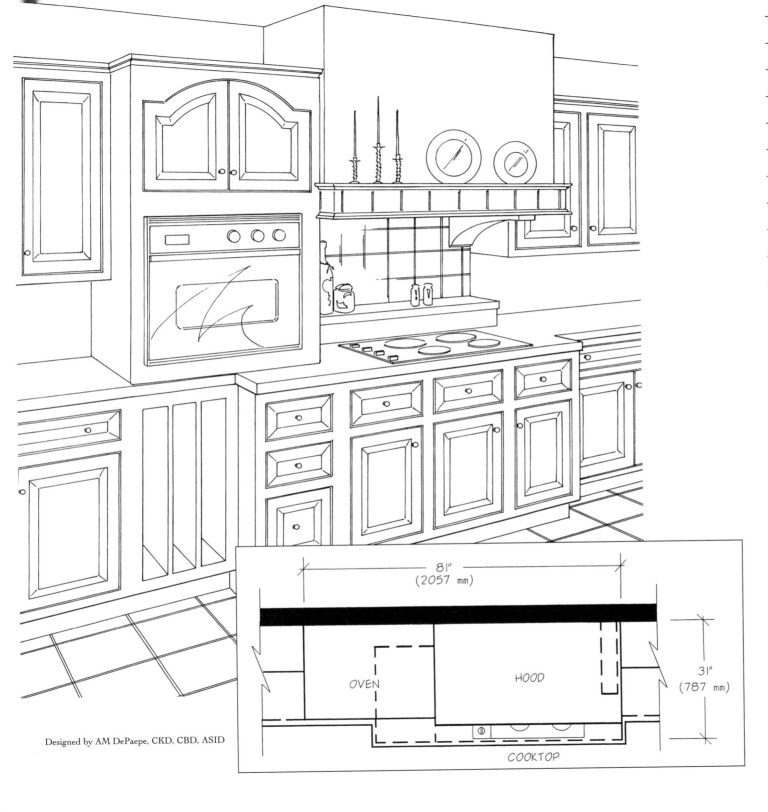

This asymmetrical design combines traditional charm with modern convenience. A 33"-wide x 48"-high x 24"-deep cabinet is customized with two arched doors and space to hold a single wall oven 37 1/2" above the floor. Below this cabinet is a 15"-wide open tray divider and a 15"-wide three-drawer base, which is pulled out to 30" deep. A 48"-wide base cabinet with three equal-sized doors and drawers houses the 30" cooktop. A 6"-high, 6"-deep, 48"-long shelf creates a backsplash for the cooktop and grounds the decorative tile and custom hood above. The hood is surfaced in drywall and measures 48" wide, 26" deep and 30" high. Along its bottom, a 4" tile border is edged with 1" moldings. Extending the border 3" from the hood creates a shallow display shelf.

Designed by AM DePaepe, CKD, CBD, ASID

81"
(2057 mm)

31"
(787 mm)

OVEN

HOOD

COOKTOP

The Aga Cooker takes center stage in any work station because of its unique design and large size. Measuring 58 1/2" wide, it features 10 cooking functions. The extra-large appliance is balanced by proportionally massive architectural elements with simple details. The cooker shown here is housed in a 111"-wide x 21"-deep niche. Much like a fireplace, the area is framed using broad 9" moldings with beaded edge details. It is topped with a buildup of crown moldings, which create the look of a mantel.

Designed by AM DePaepe,
CKD, CBD, ASID
Range, Aga

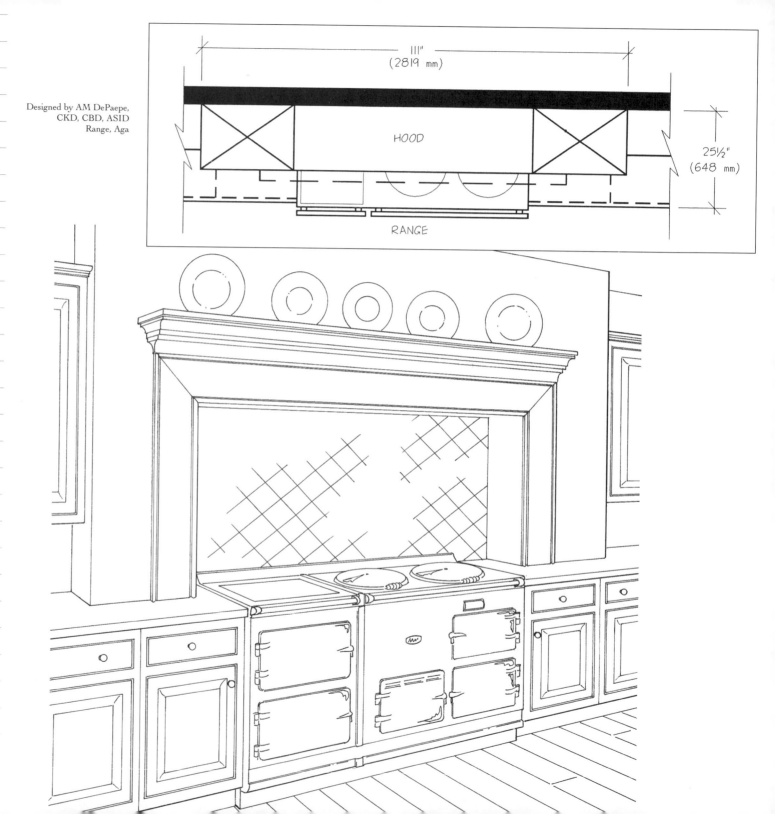

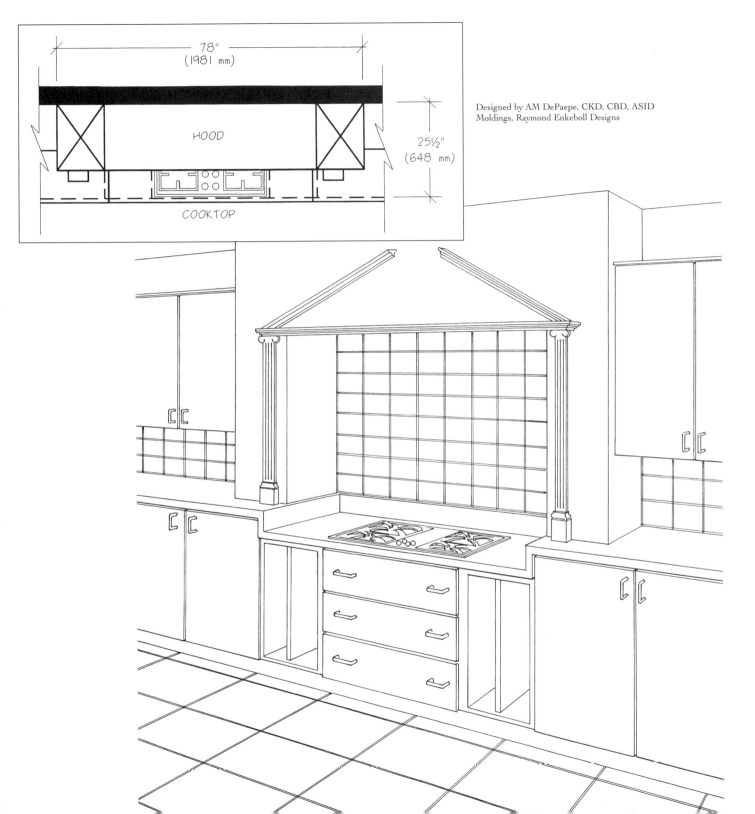

78"
(1981 mm)

HOOD

25½"
(648 mm)

COOKTOP

Designed by AM DePaepe, CKD, CBD, ASID
Moldings, Raymond Enkeboll Designs

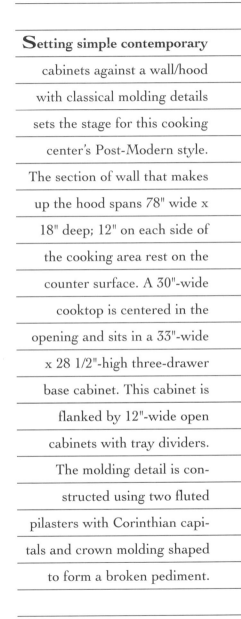

Setting simple contemporary cabinets against a wall/hood with classical molding details sets the stage for this cooking center's Post-Modern style. The section of wall that makes up the hood spans 78" wide x 18" deep; 12" on each side of the cooking area rest on the counter surface. A 30"-wide cooktop is centered in the opening and sits in a 33"-wide x 28 1/2"-high three-drawer base cabinet. This cabinet is flanked by 12"-wide open cabinets with tray dividers. The molding detail is constructed using two fluted pilasters with Corinthian capitals and crown molding shaped to form a broken pediment.

Simple style and function

are the hallmarks of this cook-

ing center. The 80"-wide span

holds two 18"-wide modular

cooking units, each with its

own downdraft vent. The units

are separated by an expanse of

countertop that features built-

in stainless steel rods. Sitting in

custom routs carved into the

solid surface counter, the rods

provide a place to rest hot

pans. Other stainless steel

details include pullout racks in

the center base cabinet, the two

3" columns that appear to sup-

port the unit and a 72" x 24"

utensil hanging grid on the

backsplash. The cabinets con-

sist of three 24"-wide bases and

three 24"-wide x 24"-high wall

cabinets. Defined by 4" fillers

on either side, the wall cabinets

are pulled forward 6" from the

room's adjacent cabinets.

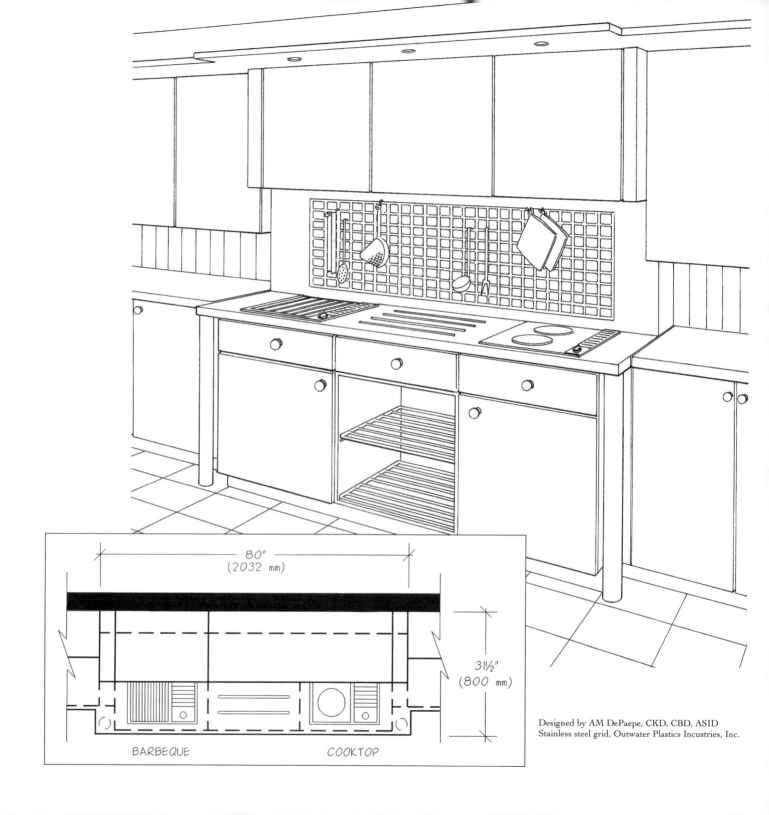

80"
(2032 mm)

3 11/2"
(800 mm)

BARBEQUE   COOKTOP

Designed by AM DePaepe, CKD, CBD, ASID
Stainless steel grid, Outwater Plastics Incustries, Inc.

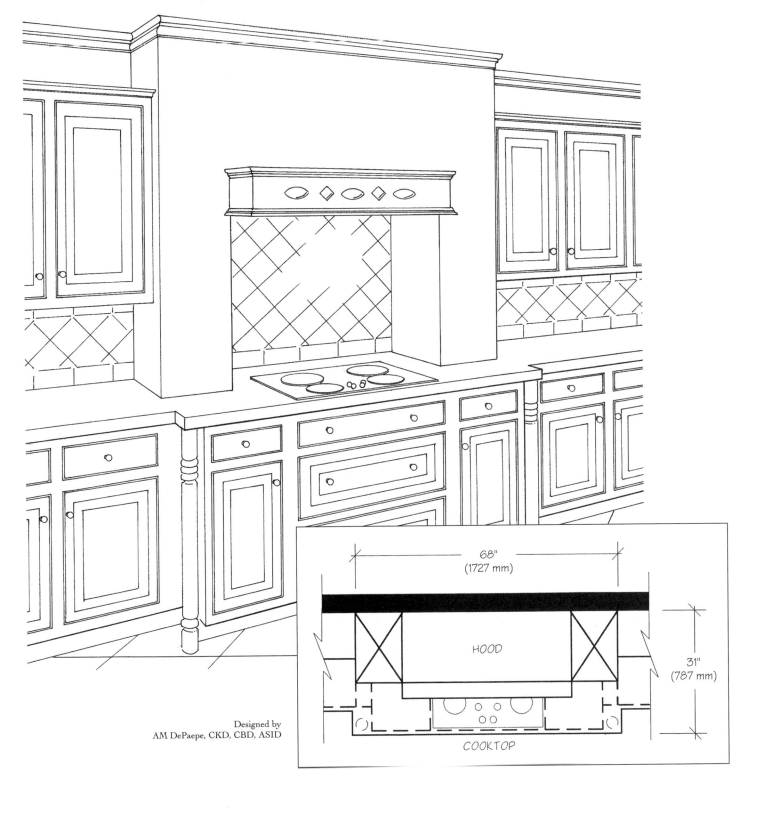

Designed by
AM DePaepe, CKD, CBD, ASID

68"
(1727 mm)

HOOD

31"
(787 mm)

COOKTOP

Concealed inside the architectural wall segment that frames the cooktop, this cooking center's hood is 69" wide x 18" deep and has an opening that is 45" wide x 36" high. The top of the opening is crowned with a cut-out valance extended 6" from the hood. This both forms a decorative shelf and facilitates the ventilation process. The base cabinets are pulled away from the back wall 6" and framed on either side by 3" colonial balusters. Inserting two 4"-wide fillers or extended stiles onto the adjacent 24"-deep base cabinets provides the space to accommodate the balusters. The base cabinets consist of a 30"-wide, three-drawer cooktop base between two 15"-wide units.

Professional cooking equipment is aesthetically integrated into its residential surroundings using traditionally-styled wood cabinets. The 48"-wide freestanding range features six burners, two ovens and a 5"-high backsplash. The appliance is framed by two 9"-wide cabinets; one equipped with a pullout rack to store spices, the other designed to accommodate trays. A custom stainless steel hood measures 54" wide x 24" deep and extends to the 9' ceiling. On either side of the hood, 6"-wide sections of wall are supported by large curving corbels. A cantilevered shelf between the corbels sits approximately 12" above the cooking surface, providing convenient open storage for cooking oils and spices.

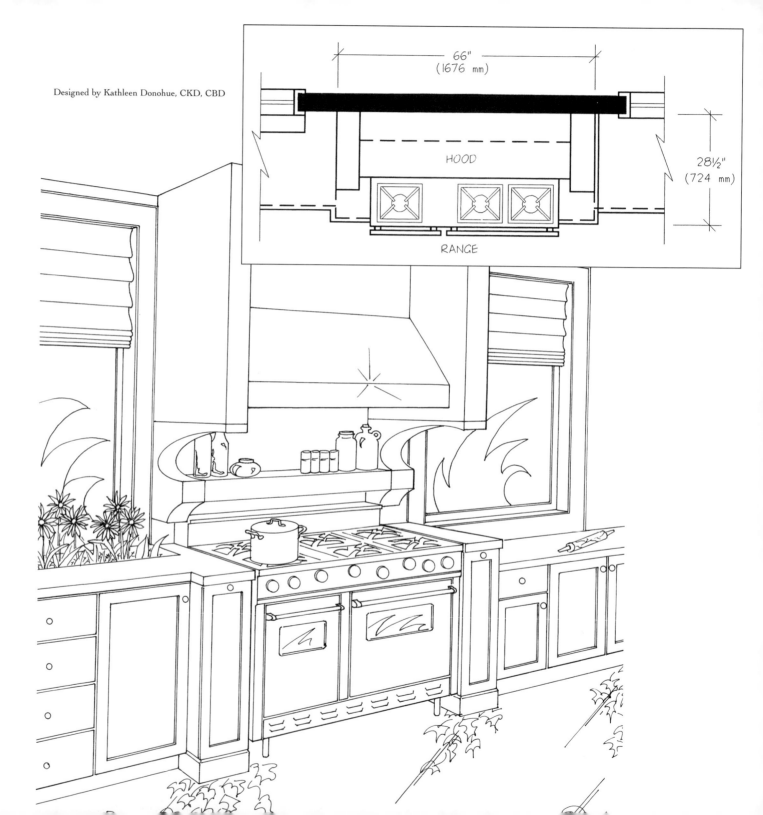

Designed by Kathleen Donohue, CKD, CBD

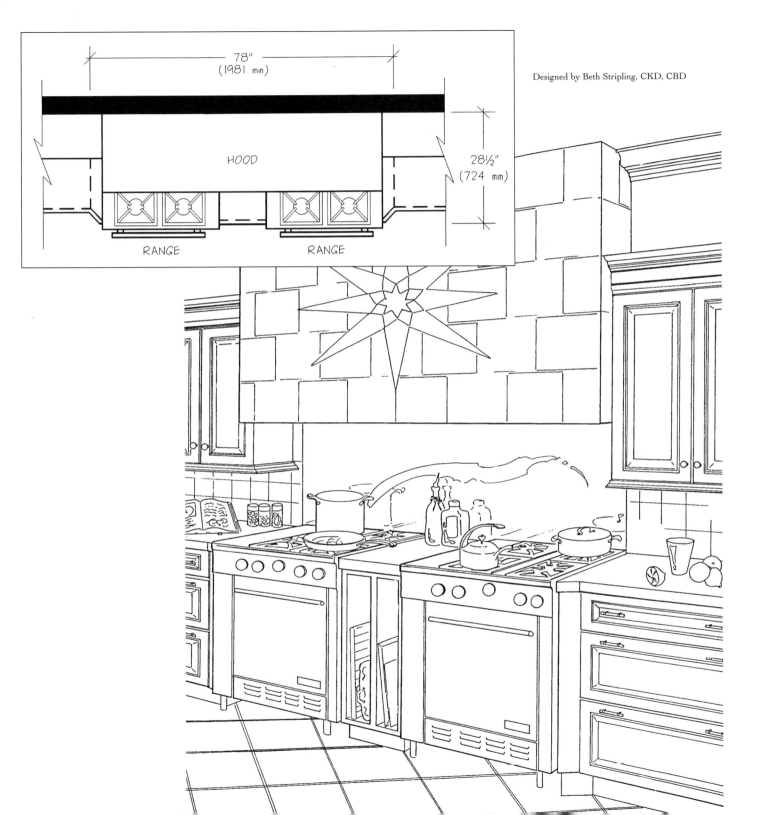

78"
(1981 mm)

HOOD

28½"
(724 mm)

RANGE   RANGE

Designed by Beth Stripling, CKD, CBD

A **certain attention getter,** this cooking center is designed for maximum impact. Your eye is immediately drawn to the massive custom hood, which is 72" wide, 21" deep and extends straight up to the 9' ceiling. The hood is surfaced in contrasting tiles that are cut to create a large decorative star at its center, further emphasizing the architectural impression. The dramatic look is continued with a stainless steel backsplash below, which contrasts with the adjacent tile backsplash. Two 30"-wide freestanding ranges are separated by a 12"-wide open tray divider pulled to 27" deep. Angled 3" fillers horizontally tie the cooking center to the 24"-deep base cabinets located to their right and left.

Arts & Crafts styling

shines through the details in this cooking center. The professional cooking range, featuring six burners and an oven, measures 36" wide x 28 1/2" deep. To create an integrated look with such a deep range, 3"-wide fillers accented with chamfered corner details were extended on either side. To the outside of each filler is a 15"-wide base cabinet. Above, a 36"-wide metal hood extends through an open shelf cabinet. Set off by two tiny wooden brackets, the 12"-high x 15"-deep open cabinet hangs 6" above adjacent 18"-wide x 30"-high wall cabinets with inset doors and a dual panel design. Together, these three cabinets form a cohesive frame for the range and hood.

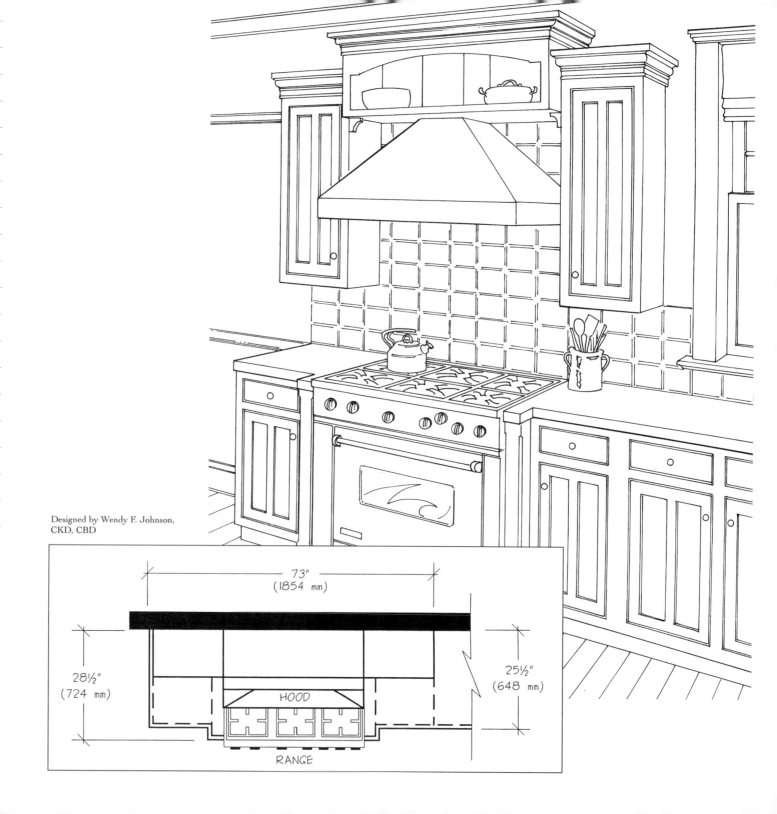

Designed by Wendy F. Johnson, CKD, CBD

73"
(1854 mm)

28½"
(724 mm)

25½"
(648 mm)

HOOD

RANGE

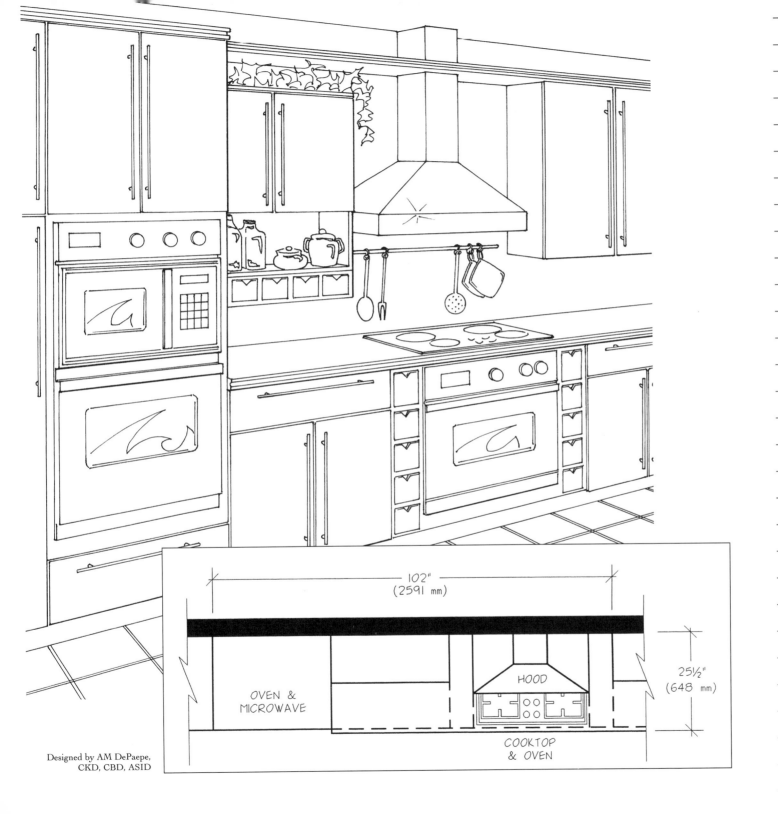

Designed by AM DePaepe,
CKD, CBD, ASID

102"
(2591 mm)

25½"
(648 mm)

OVEN &
MICROWAVE

HOOD

COOKTOP
& OVEN

This 102"-wide cooking center accommodates a bevy of appliances: oven, cooktop and microwave/wall oven combination unit. On the far left, a 30"-wide x 90"-high tall cabinet holds the micro/oven combination. Next, a 30"-wide base cabinet allows for counter surface and storage between the ovens and cooktop. A 30"-wide x 30"-high wall cabinet has 12" of open storage and a 6"-high row of apothecary drawers. The 30" cooktop and oven are set between 6"-wide columns of apothecary drawers—ideal for adding an extra pinch of spice during the cooking process. The 30"-wide hood is kept 6" away from the adjacent wall cabinets, providing the opportunity to extend a contrasting backsplash material from the counter to the soffit board.

Traditional details are combined with modern technology in this gracious cooking center. Attention is focused on the large custom hood that spans the 91" length of the center. The hood is supported by decorative wood corbels set against two 6"-wide perpendicular walls that protrude 13". The corbels extend another 8", making the total depth of the hood 21". A molding buildup then creates a mantel across the face. A row of base cabinets is sandwiched between two 6"-wide filler/return panels pulled to 30" deep and adorned with two chamfered corners. Two 15"-wide, four-drawer units flank two 30"-wide undercounter ovens, which are separated by a 1" filler strip. A 36" cooktop, featuring four burners and a griddle, is centered above the ovens.

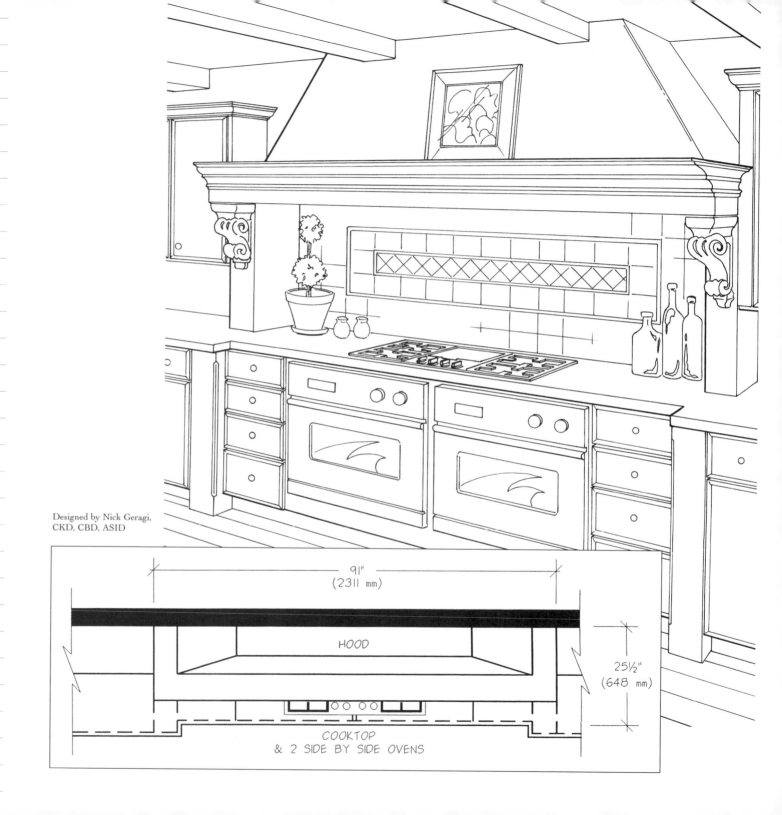

Designed by Nick Geragi,
CKD, CBD, ASID

91"
(2311 mm)

HOOD

25½"
(648 mm)

COOKTOP
& 2 SIDE BY SIDE OVENS

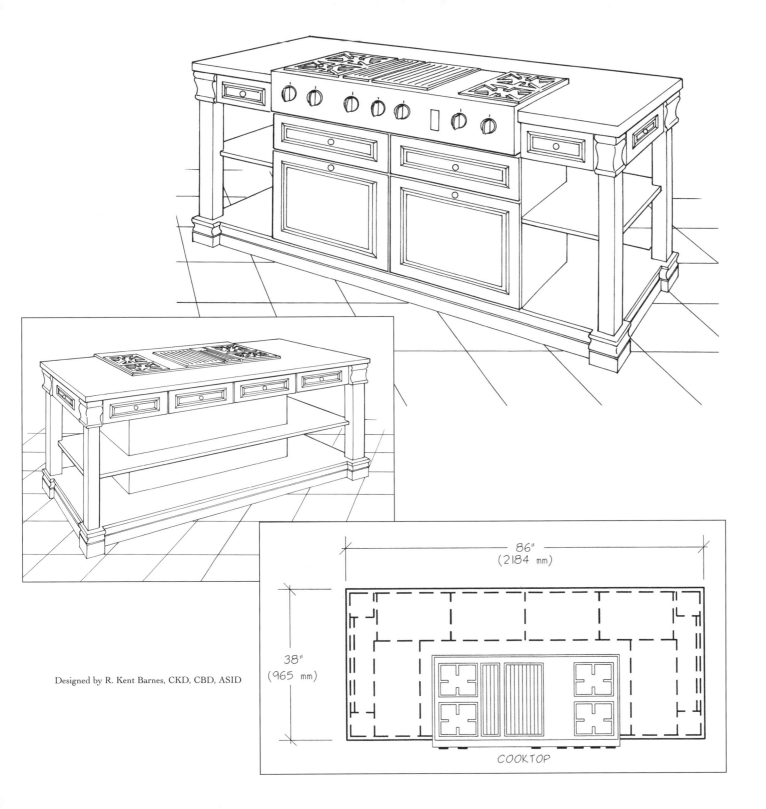

Designed by R. Kent Barnes, CKD, CBD, ASID

86"
(2184 mm)

38"
(965 mm)

COOKTOP

This furniture-look work table/island makes an appealing cooking center. Drawers wrap the apron area, interrupted only by a professional 48"-wide cooktop at the island's center. The four corners are accentuated by column-like structures that effortlessly tie into the baseboard and apron molding. Below the cooktop is a 48"-wide, 27"-high base cabinet that features four drawers— shallow at the top and deep at the bottom. The remaining storage consists of open shelving that wraps its way around the cooktop and its base, creating one shelf at the center and another at the baseboard.

This cooking center is built right into the architectural space of the home. The walls project into the room to form a 24"-deep base that accommodates a 30" cooktop and a 30" wall oven. An open arch below the cooktop is equipped with a pullout stainless steel rack; the counter's front edge features a metal rail for hanging utensils and pot holders. Above the counter, the wall section projects a more shallow 12" into the room. It includes ventilation for the cooktop, space for a 24"-wide x 12"-high built-in microwave and an arched storage niche. The textured wall surface angles out above the cooktop, forming the shape of a traditional hood. This is accented with crown molding at the bottom and top.

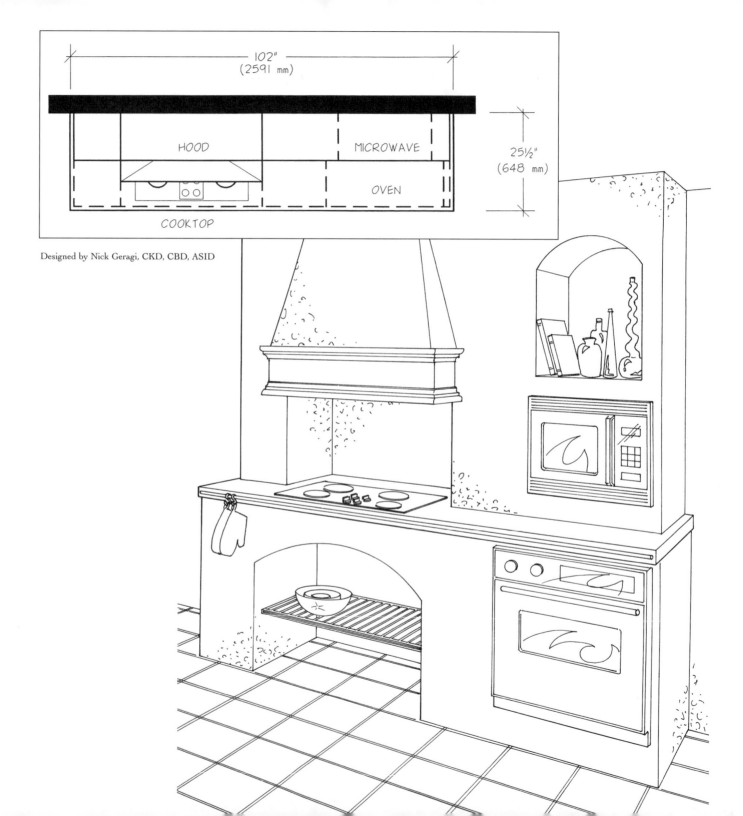

Designed by Nick Geragi, CKD, CBD, ASID

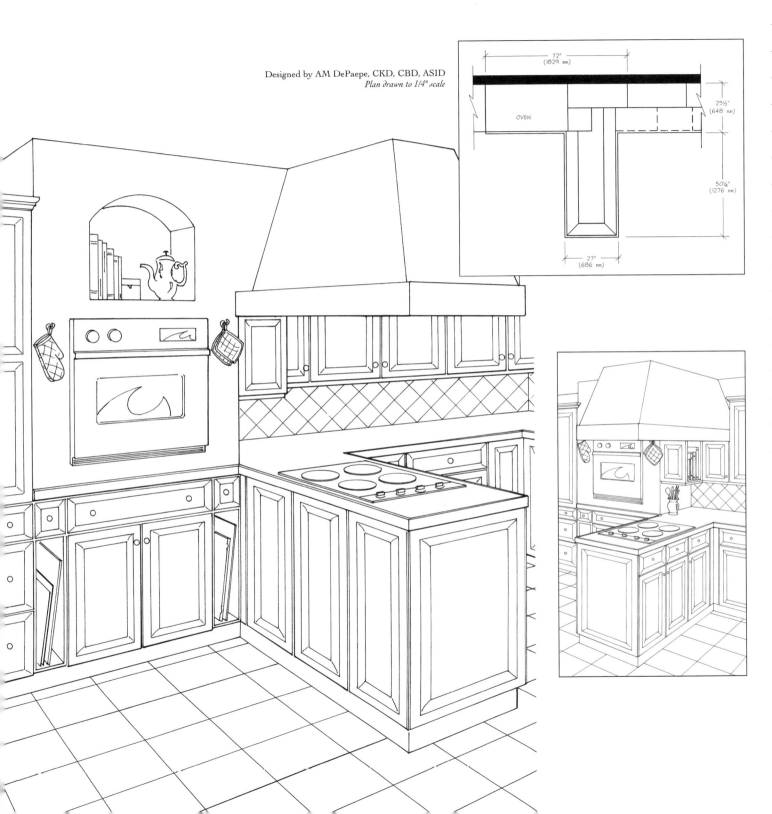

Designed by AM DePaepe, CKD, CBD, ASID
Plan drawn to 1/4" scale

72"
(1829 mm)

25½"
(648 mm)

OVEN

50¼"
(1276 mm)

27"
(686 mm)

This cooking peninsula allows two cooks to share a single cooktop without stepping on each other's toes. The cooktop is housed in a 48"-wide base that is connected to the other cabinetry with a 1 1/2"-wide filler. One side of the peninsula base has three equal doors and drawers, while the other is finished with three false doors. A large custom hood extends over the entire cooktop area. The 15"-high wall cabinets intersect with the hood at the right of the cooktop, providing a combination of open and closed storage. At the back of the peninsula, an oven is built into a 24"-deep wall area that sits directly atop the counter. Cabinets below the wall include a 30"-wide base flanked by 6"-wide tray divider cabinets topped with small apothecary drawers.

Despite its average size, this cooking center has no trouble exceeding the norm. The key is in the visual expansion of the hood area: Continuing the tile border with beaded paneling and molding details for 15" on either side of the 36"-wide hood forms a generous mantel-like shelf. The base cabinets consist of a 15"-wide, four-drawer unit to the left, a 36"-wide cooktop base in the middle and a 15"-wide door and drawer unit to the right. The border on the backsplash, which spans the center's full 67 1/2" width and 36" height, also helps to create the illusion of a much larger space.

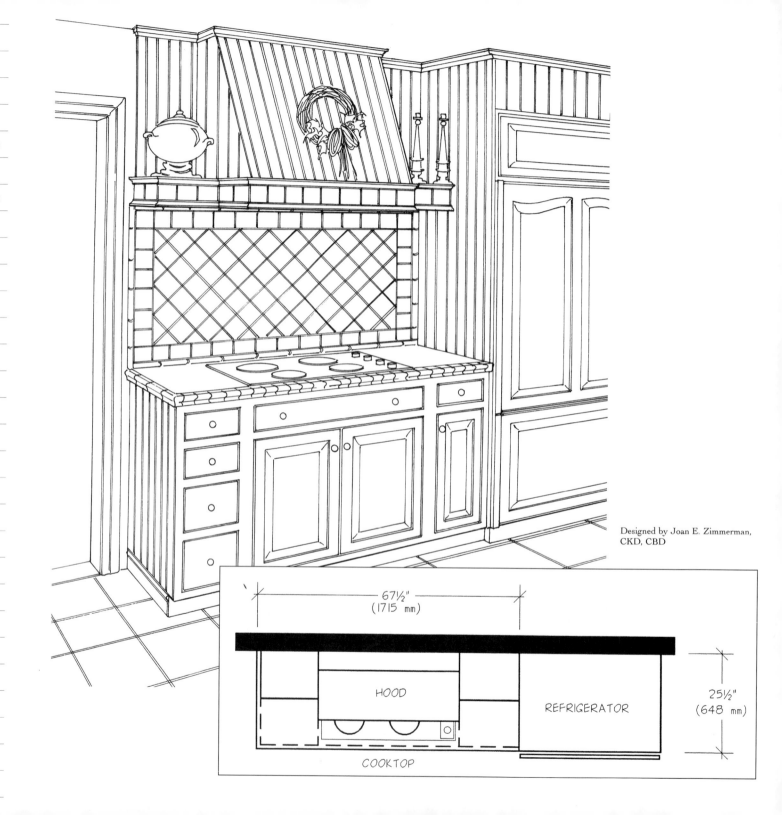

Designed by Joan E. Zimmerman, CKD, CBD

67½"
(1715 mm)

HOOD

REFRIGERATOR

25½"
(648 mm)

COOKTOP

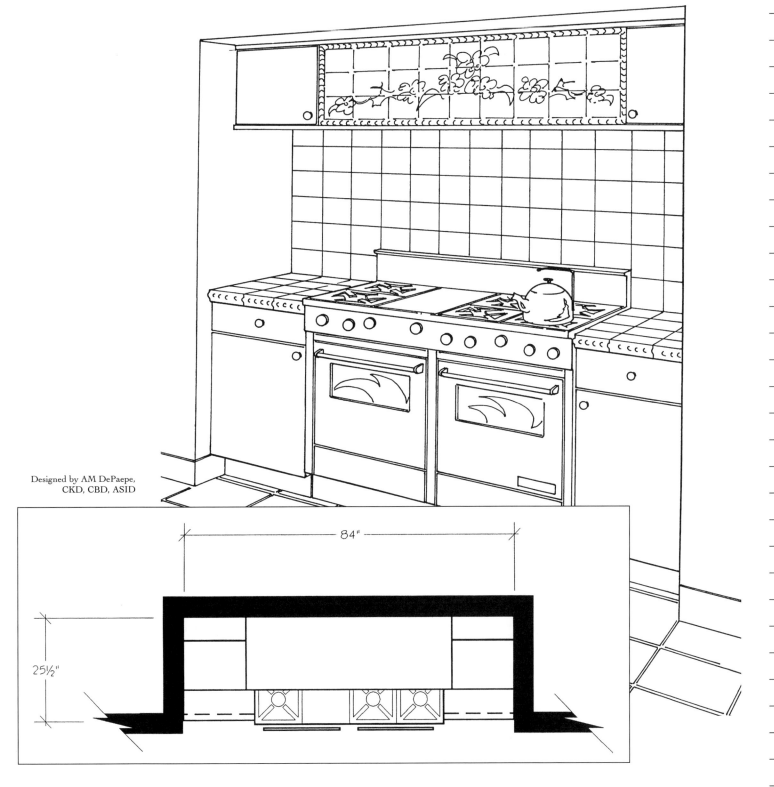

Designed by AM DePaepe,
CKD, CBD, ASID

84"

25½"

This cooking center is designed to help blend professional-style cooking equipment into more tradition- al surroundings. The 48"-wide range is set against intimate rope details, located at the edge of the tile countertop and around the custom hood. The hood, designed with a flat, tiled face, aligns with 15"-wide x 15"-high wall cabinets. Framing the wall around the entire center also influences the perceived scale. The range, which features two ovens and six gas burners, is flanked by 18"-wide base cabinets.

CHAPTER THREE

Preparation Centers

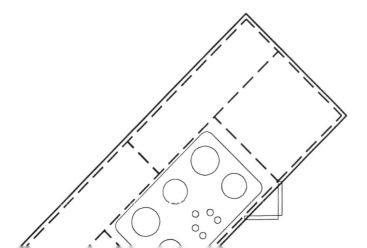

This Arts & Crafts-style
kitchen features a deceptively
modern preparation counter,
which spans from the diagonally placed sink to the built-in
refrigerator. The 84"-wide x
28"-deep work surface is highlighted by a tile backsplash
with a 54"-wide arched nook.
Above the nook are 30"-wide
x 24"-high wall cabinets with
glass doors. On either side are
30"-wide x 36"-high x 15"-deep
wall cabinets, which help to
frame a display area backed
with beaded board. The cabinet above the sink is open at
the bottom, providing easy
access to cookbooks. Base
storage for the center begins
below the sink with a 36"-wide
diagonal corner cabinet. This is
followed by a 21"-wide pullout
waste basket, a 42"-wide double drawer/door unit, and a
21"-wide four-drawer base.

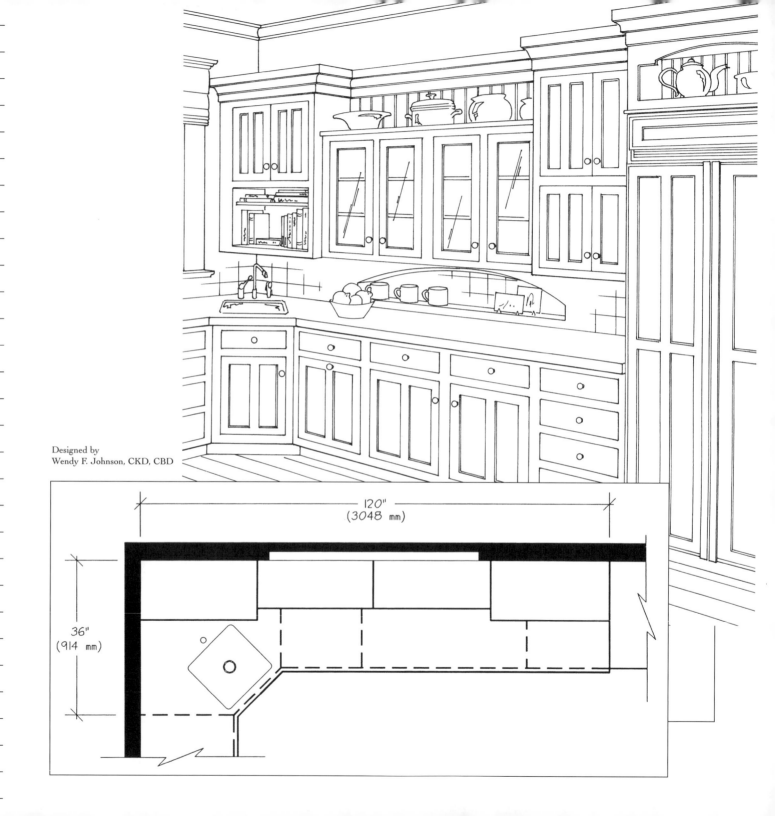

Designed by
Wendy F. Johnson, CKD, CBD

Designed by Mary Jo Peterson,
CKD, CBD for GE Appliances

90¾"
(2305 mm)

MICROWAVE

D/W

Universal access is the hallmark of this preparation area, which is centered around a 42"-wide x 30"-high work surface with a small sink and kneespace for a seated worker. Throughout the kitchen, the toekicks are raised to 12" to provide space for the feet of a person using a wheelchair. This results in a raised dishwasher at the right—convenient for individuals of all abilities. At the left, the second drawerhead of the 24"-wide, four-drawer base has a pullout work surface that is cut out to hold a mixing bowl. The countertop surfaces above the stock base cabinet and standard dishwasher are 41" above the floor. The 30"-high wall cabinets above consist of one 42"-wide and two 24"-wide units that are either open or have glass doors so items can be easily located.

When space is tight, a secondary preparation center can move to a wall all its own. This one is tucked between two 18"-wide x 12"-deep tall cabinets that feature a glass door at the top, appliance garage and apothecary drawers at the mid-section, and a 36"-high door at the bottom. The 42"-high work surface rests on two 12"-wide base cabinets before it curves out to form a 24"-wide x 21"-deep station suitable for a standing user of average height, or for a person seated on a bar stool. The 48"-wide x 30"-high wall space above is fitted with an organization system that features hooks for utensils, cutlery, cookbooks, etc. A 12"-high x 48"-wide open shelf for bulk grain storage runs across the top.

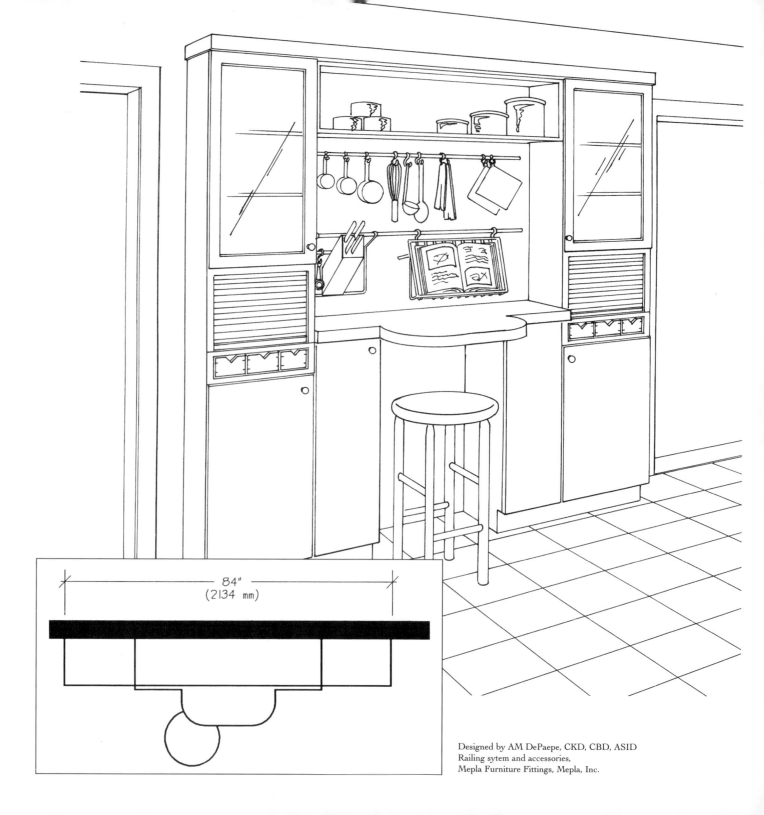

84"
(2134 mm)

Designed by AM DePaepe, CKD, CBD, ASID
Railing sytem and accessories,
Mepla Furniture Fittings, Mepla, Inc.

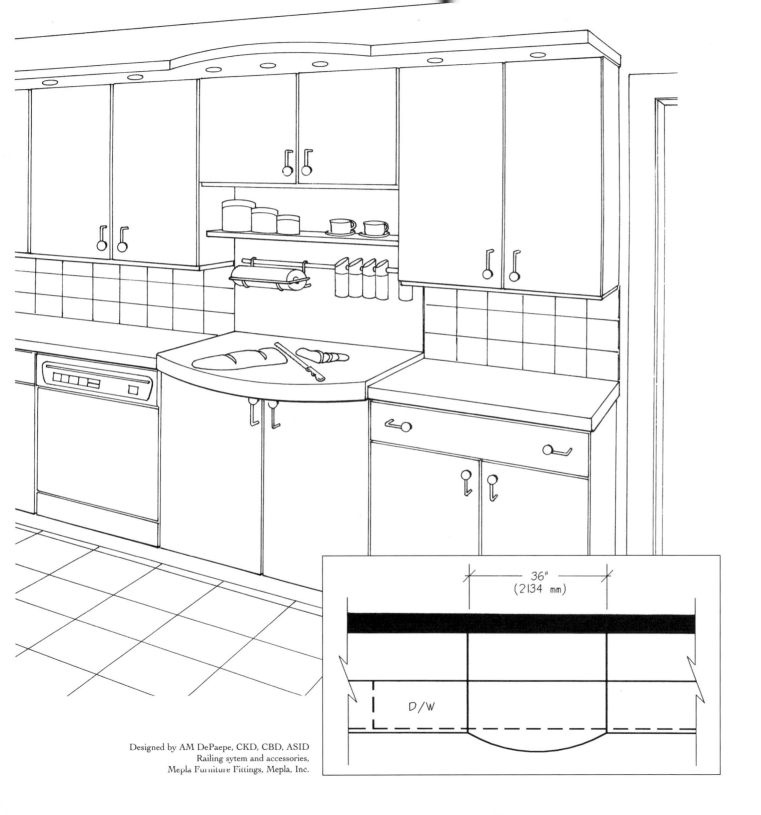

Designed by AM DePaepe, CKD, CBD, ASID
Railing sytem and accessories,
Mepla Furniture Fittings, Mepla, Inc.

The small 36"-wide preparation center illustrated here will become a focal point of any kitchen. Its design employs three strategies to emphasize the area: changing the material and thickness of the work surface and protruding its front edge toward the user in a shallow curve; contrasting the backsplash material; and curving the soffit board to match the shape of the counter edge. The base cabinet has two full-height doors, since a top drawer would be hindered by the counter protrusion. Above, a 15"-high wall cabinet leaves plenty of room for a 33"-high backsplash. A 9"-deep shelf is mounted 9" below the wall cabinet bottom. Suspended from a single rail hung 6" below the shelf are a handy paper towel holder and multiple spice containers.

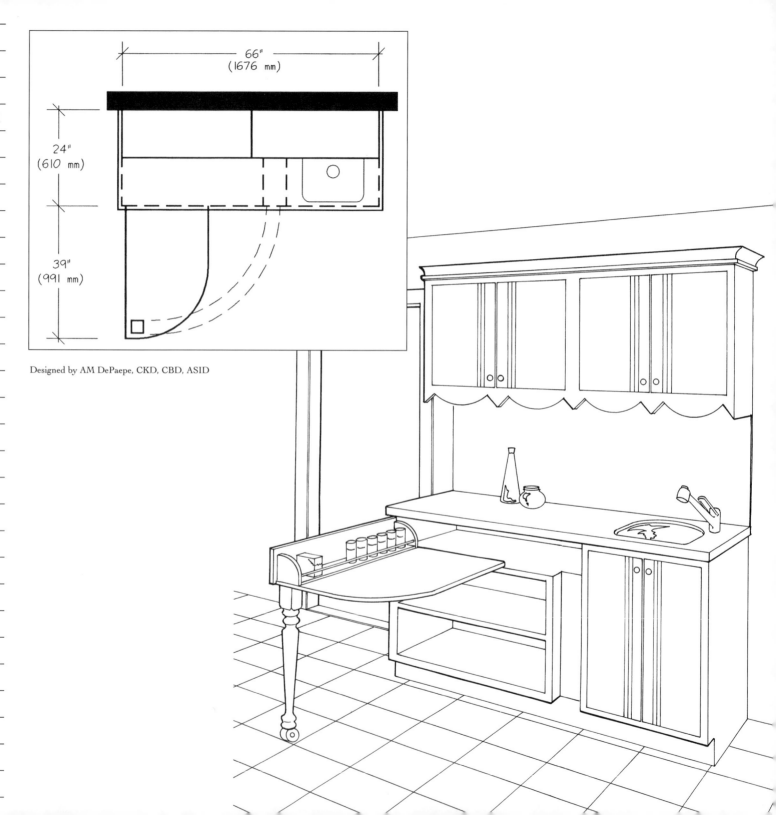

Designed by AM DePaepe, CKD, CBD, ASID

An eclectic mix of whimsical and traditional details highlight this expandable preparation center, shown in its open position. The left base cabinet is 42" wide. Its top drawerhead is attached to a work surface that swings out 90 degrees and holds spices along its back edge. When the counter is closed, the Colonial-style balustrade fits neatly into 6" of filler that is set back 6" from the face. To ensure easy access when the work surface is in either position, the remaining 36" of storage in the left base cabinet is open. To the right is a standard 24"-wide sink base. Above the counter, 33"-wide x 24"-high wall cabinets are trimmed with a fun, light valance and complementary cove molding.

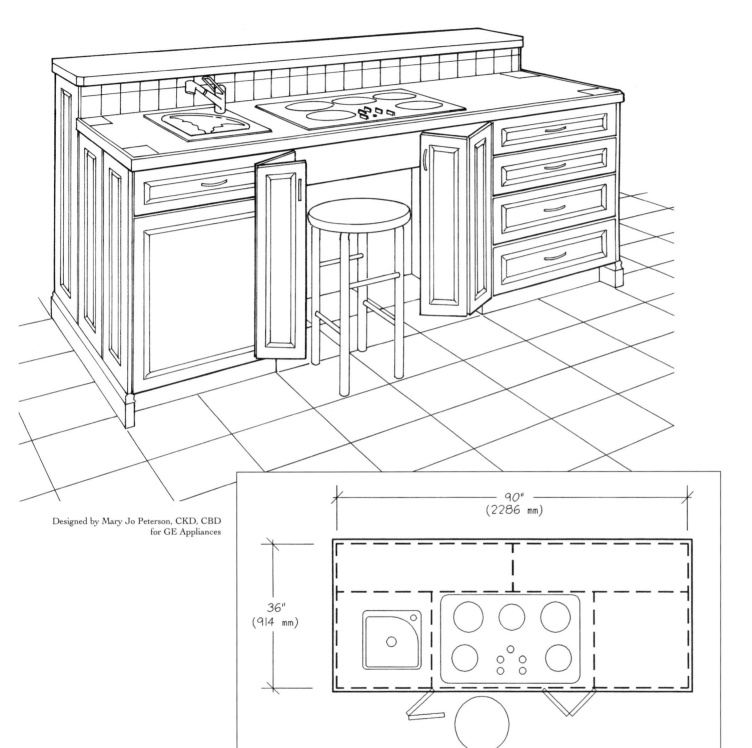

Designed by Mary Jo Peterson, CKD, CBD
for GE Appliances

90"
(2286 mm)

36"
(914 mm)

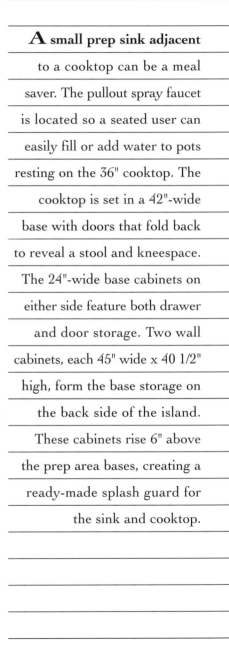

A small prep sink adjacent

to a cooktop can be a meal

saver. The pullout spray faucet

is located so a seated user can

easily fill or add water to pots

resting on the 36" cooktop. The

cooktop is set in a 42"-wide

base with doors that fold back

to reveal a stool and kneespace.

The 24"-wide base cabinets on

either side feature both drawer

and door storage. Two wall

cabinets, each 45" wide x 40 1/2"

high, form the base storage on

the back side of the island.

These cabinets rise 6" above

the prep area bases, creating a

ready-made splash guard for

the sink and cooktop.

Preparation moves to a paradise island in this kitchen design. A large 4' x 8' space provides plenty of room for people to work together. Resting on an 18"-wide base, a small prep sink is positioned near the center of the taller, 38"-high work surface. To its left is a 36"-wide base that houses a microwave; to its right is an 18"-wide pullout waste basket. Turning the corner, the counter height drops to 32". Topped with marble, this lower level provides bakers with more control for mixing and rolling dough. The attractive pot rack hanging over the island's higher level is accented with four finial-like corners that complement the base cabinets' pilaster moldings.

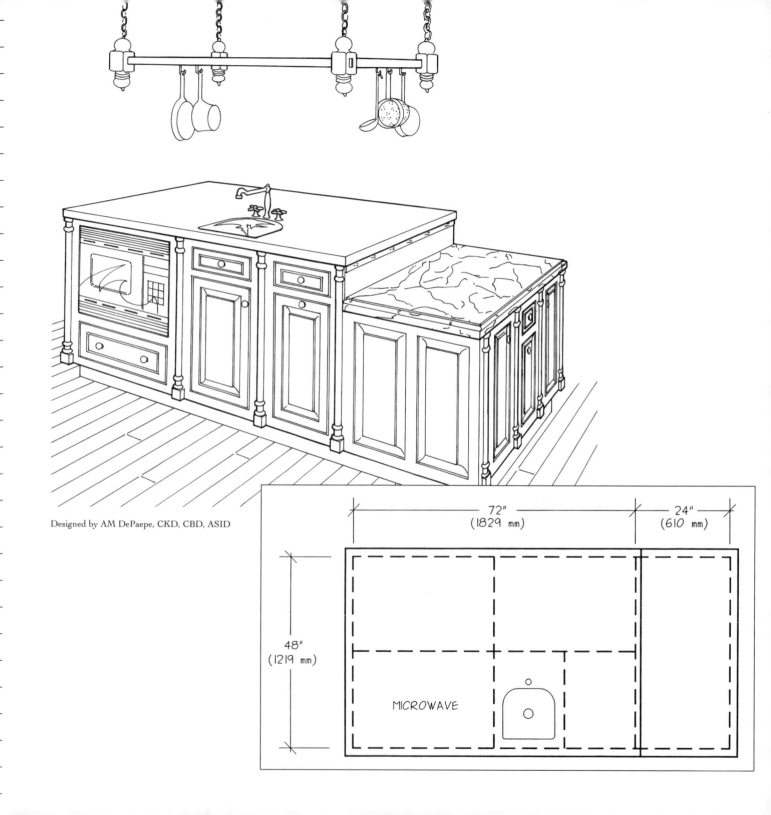

Designed by AM DePaepe, CKD, CBD, ASID

72"
(1829 mm)

24"
(610 mm)

48"
(1219 mm)

MICROWAVE

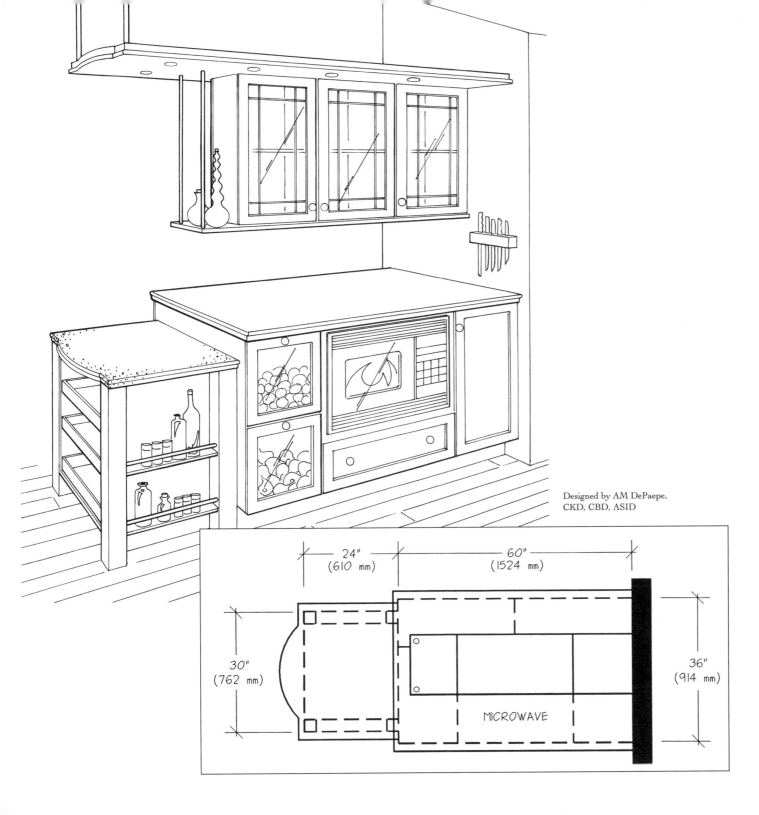

Designed by AM DePaepe,
CKD, CBD, ASID

24"
(610 mm)

60"
(1524 mm)

30"
(762 mm)

36"
(914 mm)

MICROWAVE

This multi-level peninsula provides food preparation counters for different functions, and for individuals of different heights to work together. The 36"-high taller level is made up of the following: a 15"-wide recycling bin; a 30"-wide microwave/drawer unit; a 15"-wide, two-drawer veggie bin; and two 30"-wide x 12"-deep full-height door cabinets at the back. The shorter level is a 30"-high custom base made from four 4" x 4" columns with open rollout drawers flanked by spice storage. Hung by two stainless steel rods, a soffit above follows the curved detail of the counter edge. The 15"-deep wall cabinets feature three 15"-wide glass doors on each side. A cantilevered shelf at the end of the run extends 12".

Dual kitchen helpers won't mind being marooned on this island. Its 5' x 3' work surface, designed for two individuals to face one another while preparing meals, is set off by four 6" x 6" columns at the corners. The storage area consists of two 27"-wide x 24"-deep cabinets on one side and two 27"-wide x 12"-deep cabinets on the other. The shallow cabinets illustrated in the perspective feature tilt-out storage for recyclables and veggie/grain display. The storage on the other side consists of two wide drawers at the top and four roll-out shelves hidden behind doors. Tile borders on the work surface and the floor attractively distinguish the island within the overall kitchen space.

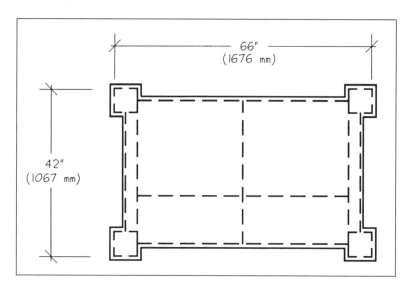

Designed by AM DePaepe, CKD, CBD, ASID

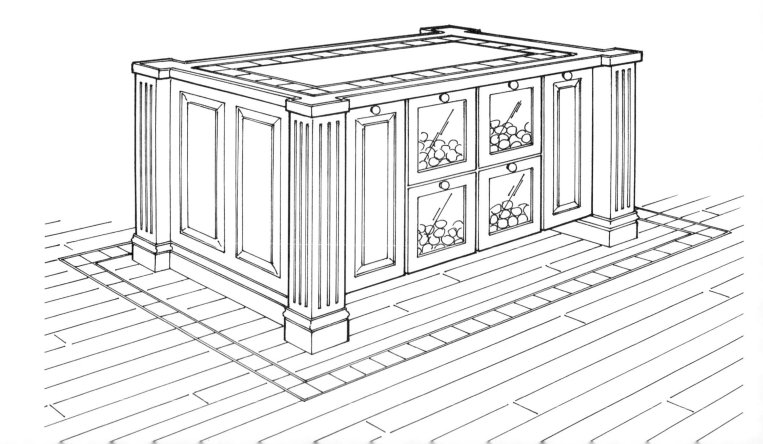

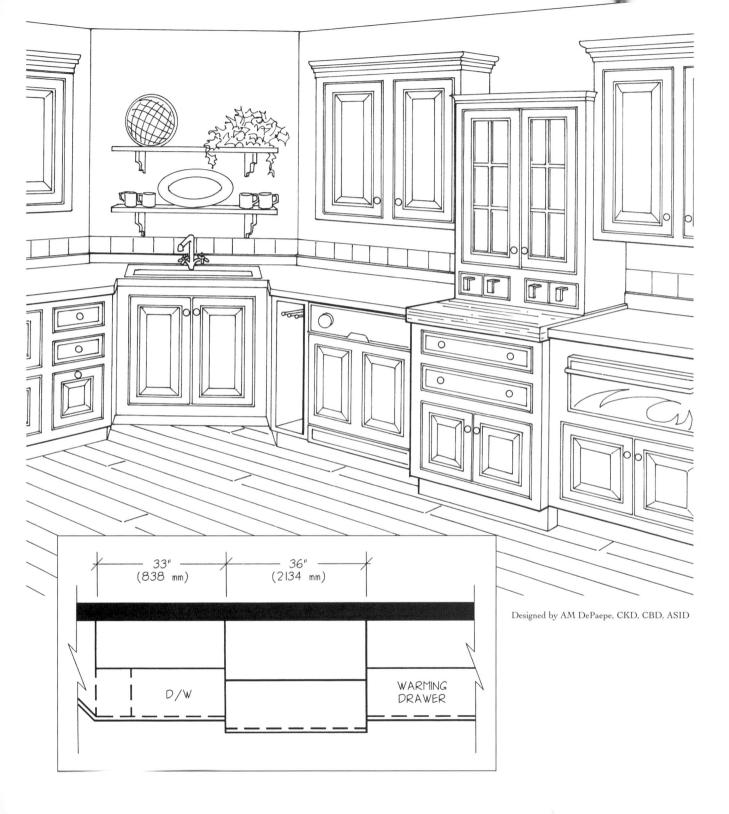

Designed by AM DePaepe, CKD, CBD, ASID

Designed to look like a separate furniture piece, this prep center complements the kitchen's traditional style. It is set apart by changes in height, depth and materials. Pulling the 36"-wide base 3" away from the back wall makes the unit appear to be 27" deep. Its butcherblock countertop is thicker than the adjacent countertop material. Above, the 36"-wide x 42"-high x 15"-deep wall cabinet features two mullioned doors sitting atop four grain cups. Resting this cabinet on the counter leaves an open display area above. On either side, 30"-high wall cabinets are hung at standard height and depth. To the left, more than 33" of 25"-deep work surface spans to a large corner sink. Below the counter are a dishwasher and a 9"-wide cabinet with pullout towel bar.

A built-in dumbwaiter is a special feature of this traditional butler's pantry. To the right of the columnar structure is storage for serving amenities such as linens and china. The two wall cabinets are each 36" wide x 60" high. To the left of the dumbwaiter is the preparation center. From right to left, its base storage includes a 9"-wide tray base, a 24" sink base, a 24" dishwasher, a 3" filler, a 24" wine chiller and another 3" filler. A 45"-wide x 42"-high wall cabinet with four mullioned glass doors holds glassware and serving pitchers above the work surface.

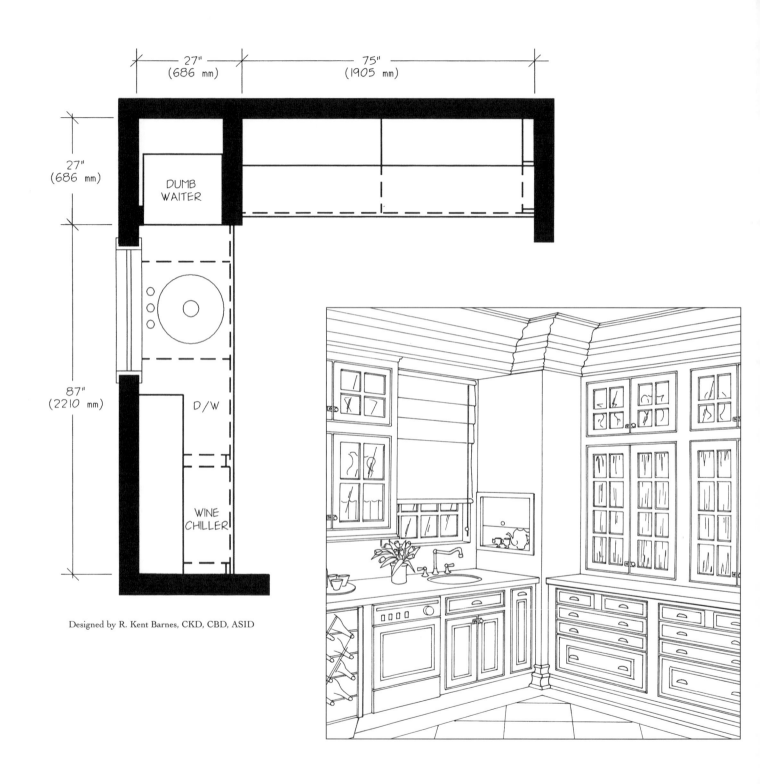

Designed by R. Kent Barnes, CKD, CBD, ASID

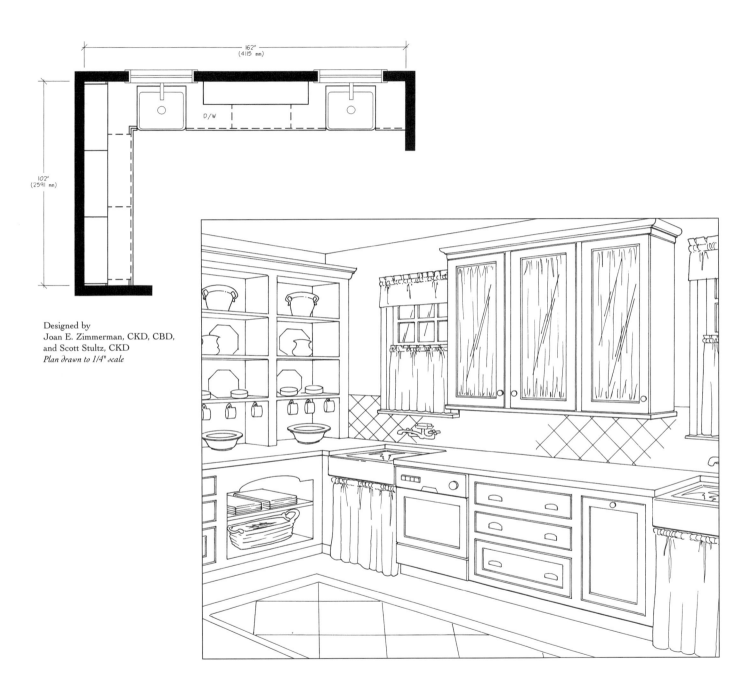

162"
(4115 mm)

102"
(2591 mm)

D/W

Designed by
Joan E. Zimmerman, CKD, CBD,
and Scott Stultz, CKD
Plan drawn to 1/4" scale

Multiple caterers can
work together in this large butler's pantry designed for modern convenience, but reminiscent of a more traditional style.
It features two 24"-wide apron-
front sinks with fabric draped
below. Between the sinks are a
dishwasher, a 30"-wide, three-
drawer base and an 18"-wide
pullout waste basket. Not
shown is a 15"-wide base,
which is located to the right of
the second sink (see plan). The
left wall is primarily used for
open storage, enabling caterers
to easily find serving dishes.
The three wall cabinets are
each 33" wide x 48" high. The
two base cabinets on this wall
are 36" wide. One is open; the
other contains three drawers
for linen storage.

This large food prep area
is similar to a butler's pantry in
look and function, but is con-
tiguous with the kitchen cabinets and work surface. The
short leg of the "L" is for storage
and display. The base cabinets
include a 36"-wide lazy susan
and a 36"-wide, five-drawer
unit. The specially-constructed
wall cabinet is 48"-wide x
48"-high with three doors and
three veggie drawers. In the
corner is a 24"-wide x 9"-deep
English Country-style open
shelf unit with apothecary
drawers and cut-out valance. A
30"-wide farmhouse-style sink is
centered on the long leg of the
"L". To its left is a dishwasher;
to its right is a 15" base and a
15" icemaker. Above the sink,
a 30"-wide x 15"-high cabinet
and a 9"-deep x 6"-high open
shelf are flanked by 36"-wide x
30"-high wall cabinets.

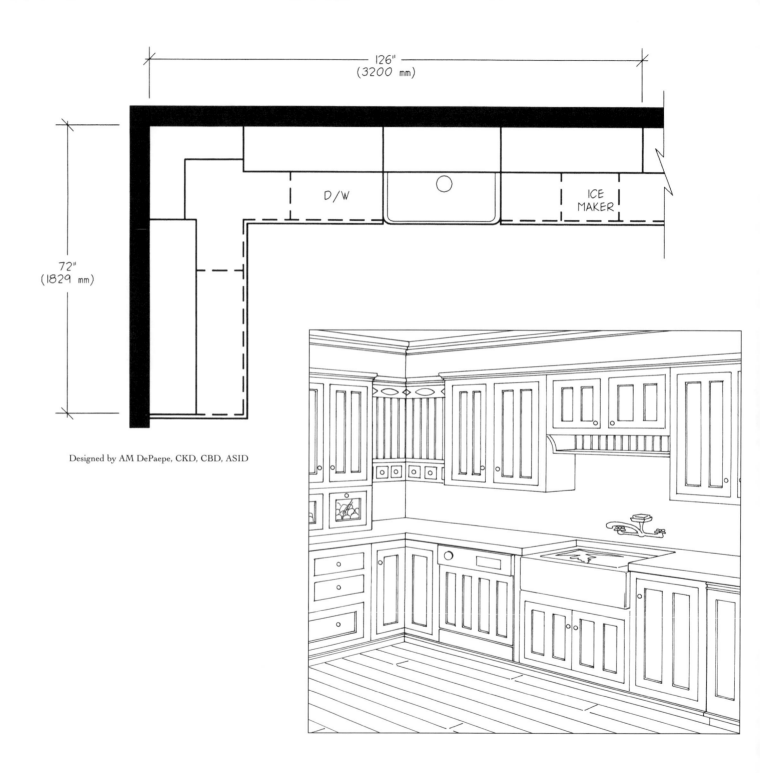

Designed by AM DePaepe, CKD, CBD, ASID

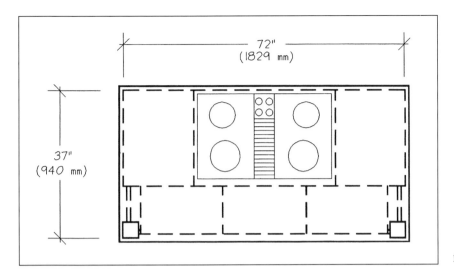

Designed by Nick Geragi, CKD, CBD, ASID

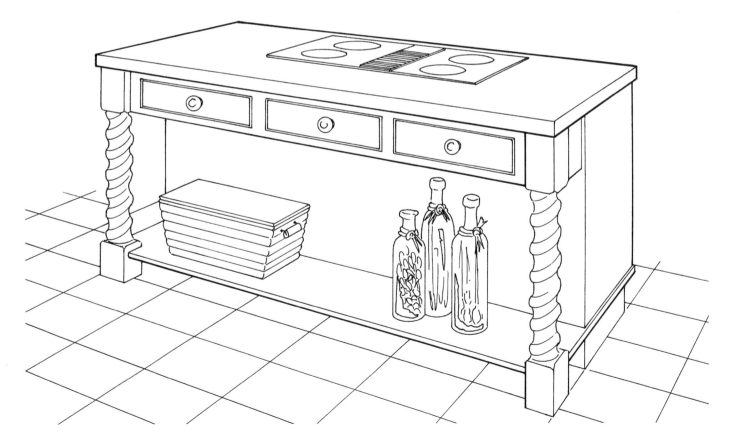

The back side of an island makes a small prep counter for a cook's helper—and an attractive transition into the eating area of the kitchen. Three 21"-wide x 6"-high drawers with extended stiles on either side fit between two turned balustrades that measure 4" square and 34 1/2" high. A shelf aligns with the molding at the top of the toekick to provide 12"-deep open storage below the drawers. The opposite side of the island consists of a 36"-wide cooktop base with an 18"-wide base cabinet on either side.

A bar sink is the heart of this drink and serving preparation center. The base cabinets (from left to right) include a 12"-wide beverage chiller; a 12"-wide, three-drawer base; a 24"-wide sink base; and a dishwasher. A 3" filler and a return panel finish the run. The wall cabinets stagger in height; the two outer ones measure 18" wide x 48" high. Each features a mullioned glass door set above four small drawers. The center wall cabinet is 36" wide x 30" high. It is designed with 1 1/2"-wide extended stiles and return panels on each end to keep the adjacent molding from interfering with the operation of the doors. Below the wall cabinet, an arched valance frames a 6" deep shelf—a perfect display space for special glassware.

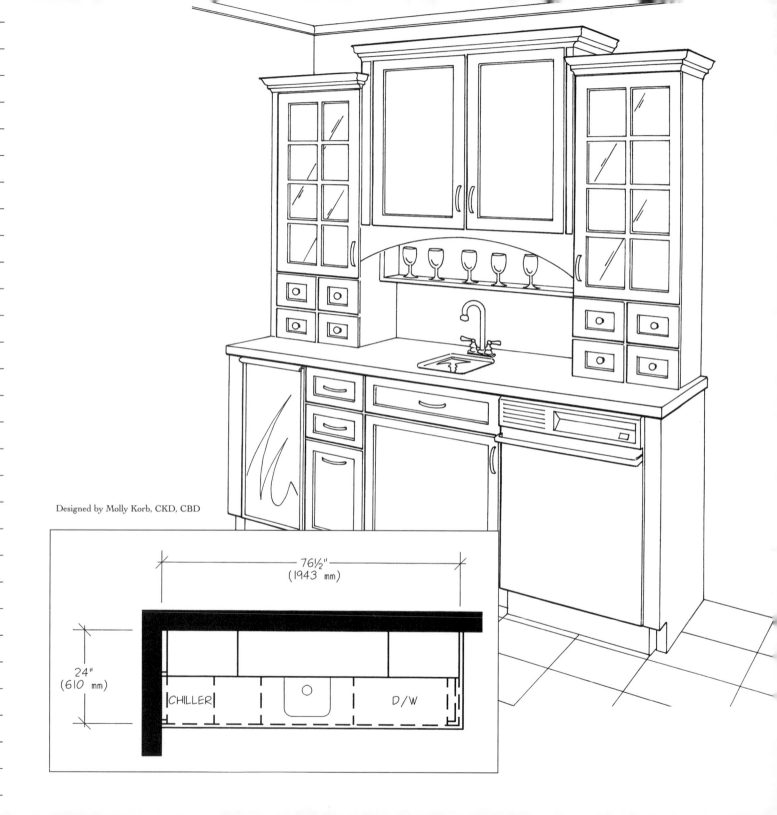

Designed by Molly Korb, CKD, CBD

76½"
(1943 mm)

24"
(610 mm)

CHILLER

D/W

Designed by AM DePaepe,
CKD, CBD, ASID

82"

26"

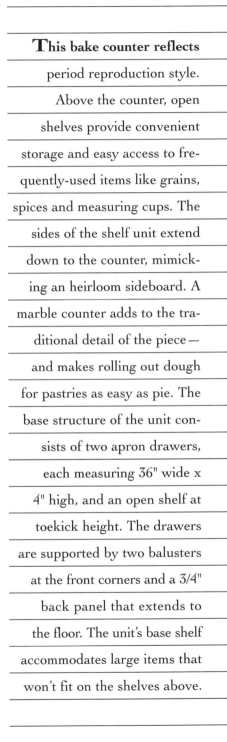

This bake counter reflects period reproduction style. Above the counter, open shelves provide convenient storage and easy access to frequently-used items like grains, spices and measuring cups. The sides of the shelf unit extend down to the counter, mimicking an heirloom sideboard. A marble counter adds to the traditional detail of the piece—and makes rolling out dough for pastries as easy as pie. The base structure of the unit consists of two apron drawers, each measuring 36" wide x 4" high, and an open shelf at toekick height. The drawers are supported by two balusters at the front corners and a 3/4" back panel that extends to the floor. The unit's base shelf accommodates large items that won't fit on the shelves above.

CHAPTER FOUR

Secondary Bake/Prep Centers

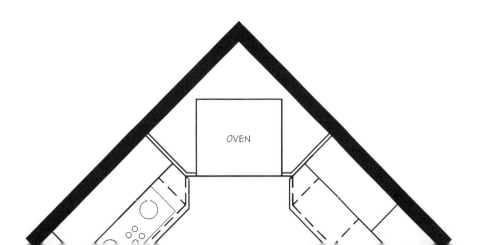

Cleverly-arranged cabinets define this work area. At its borders, 12"-wide, angle-front cabinets are pulled 12" away from the back wall. Extending two 18"-wide storage units down to the countertop sets the area apart even further. At the center, the 36"-deep counter surface tops two 9" pullout pantry units and a microwave base. The extra-deep counter provides a 24"-deep work area with storage space at the back. Beware that the center wall storage might be difficult for some users to reach; to maximize accessibility, the storage shown here was left open. An extended soffit board that mirrors the base cabinet configuration provides task lighting. The area is contained by an 18"-wide x 84"-tall pantry unit.

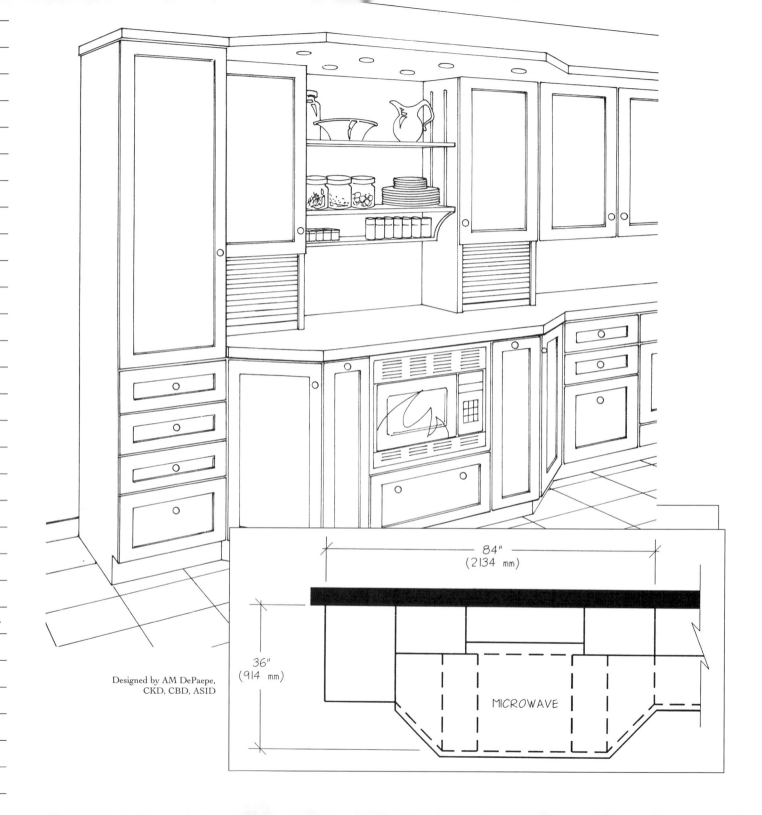

Designed by AM DePaepe,
CKD, CBD, ASID

84"
(2134 mm)

36"
(914 mm)

MICROWAVE

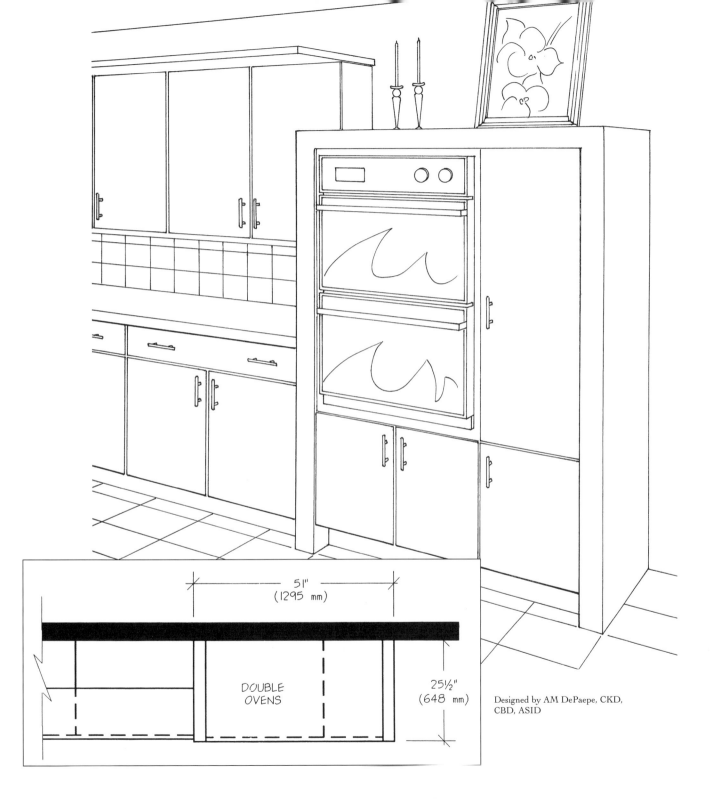

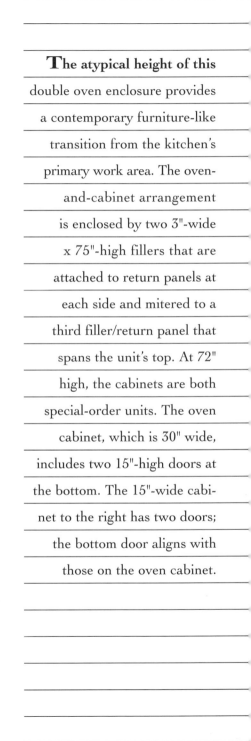

The atypical height of this double oven enclosure provides a contemporary furniture-like transition from the kitchen's primary work area. The oven-and-cabinet arrangement is enclosed by two 3"-wide x 75"-high fillers that are attached to return panels at each side and mitered to a third filler/return panel that spans the unit's top. At 72" high, the cabinets are both special-order units. The oven cabinet, which is 30" wide, includes two 15"-high doors at the bottom. The 15"-wide cabinet to the right has two doors; the bottom door aligns with those on the oven cabinet.

51"
(1295 mm)

DOUBLE
OVENS

25½"
(648 mm)

Designed by AM DePaepe, CKD, CBD, ASID

There are many times when a bake center needs to be on a separate wall from a kitchen's other work areas. In such instances it is best to provide as much counter and storage space as possible, making the area more than just a landing surface. Here, the center occupies 7' of wall space. At 30" wide x 84" high, the special-order oven/microwave cabinet has the microwave cutout at its right side, leaving a void at the front to hang a small utensil rack. Rather than the standard 30", the adjacent wall cabinet is 24" high, allowing for the new microwave location. The following 18"-wide wall cabinet compensates for lost storage by extending 48" to the countertop. Base storage includes a 36"-wide standard unit and an 18"-wide, three-drawer base.

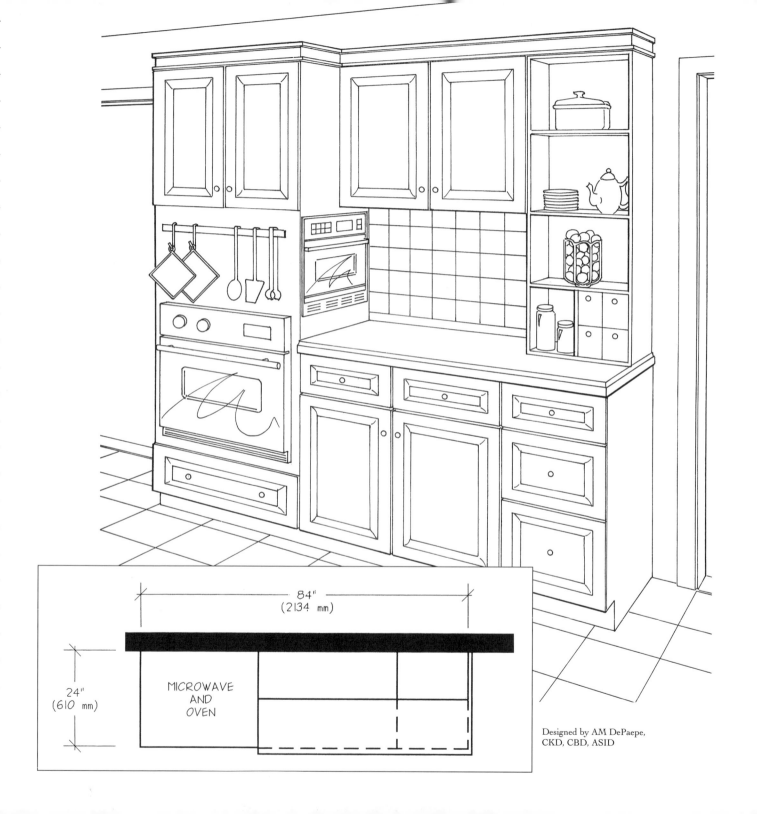

84"
(2134 mm)

24"
(610 mm)

MICROWAVE
AND
OVEN

Designed by AM DePaepe,
CKD, CBD, ASID

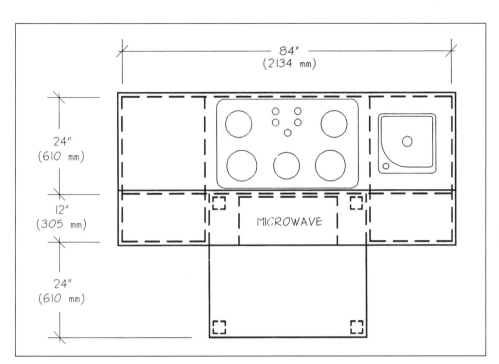

84"
(2134 mm)

24"
(610 mm)

12"
(305 mm)

MICROWAVE

24"
(610 mm)

Designed by Mary Jo Peterson, CKD, CBD
for GE Appliances

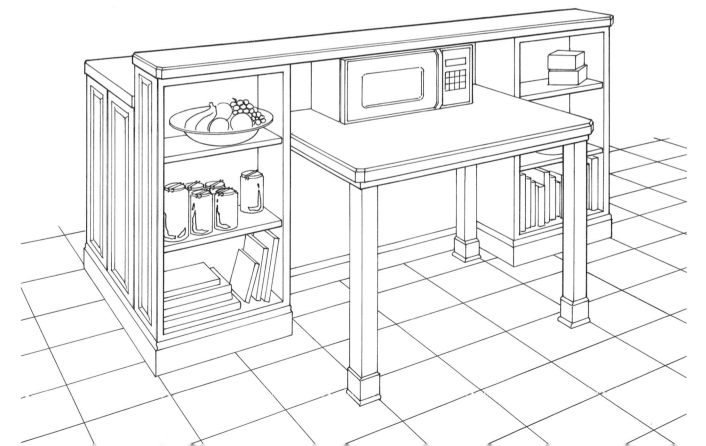

Cook's helpers get their

own work station at the back

of this island. Two 21"-wide x

12"-deep x 40 1/2"-high open

shelf cabinets make the transi-

tion from the primary cooking

center, creating both a visual

and functional barrier. Between

the two cabinets a 42"-wide

void is filled with a 30"-high

custom-made table. This leaves

just enough room for a com-

pact microwave to sit snugly

between the tabletop and the

counter. A special advantage of

this design is that the 30"-high

work surface is convenient to

use for both seated adults

and standing children.

Whether designing for a family on the go that eats in stages or for a single adult that thaws or heats leftovers for weekday meals, a second microwave adjacent to the eating area or family room is a convenient amenity. Here, the cabinet arrangement includes open space to hold books, mail and collectibles. Using 66"-high tall cabinets for the oven and open shelf unit creates a display area above. The oven cabinet measures 24" wide x 24" deep; the open shelf is 12" wide x 12" deep. Pulling out the shelf cabinet 12" from the wall allows it to be installed flush with the oven cabinet. A 24"-wide x 84"-high standard tall unit encloses the display area on the left side. The 36"-wide display shelf is highlighted by recessed lighting in the extended soffit above.

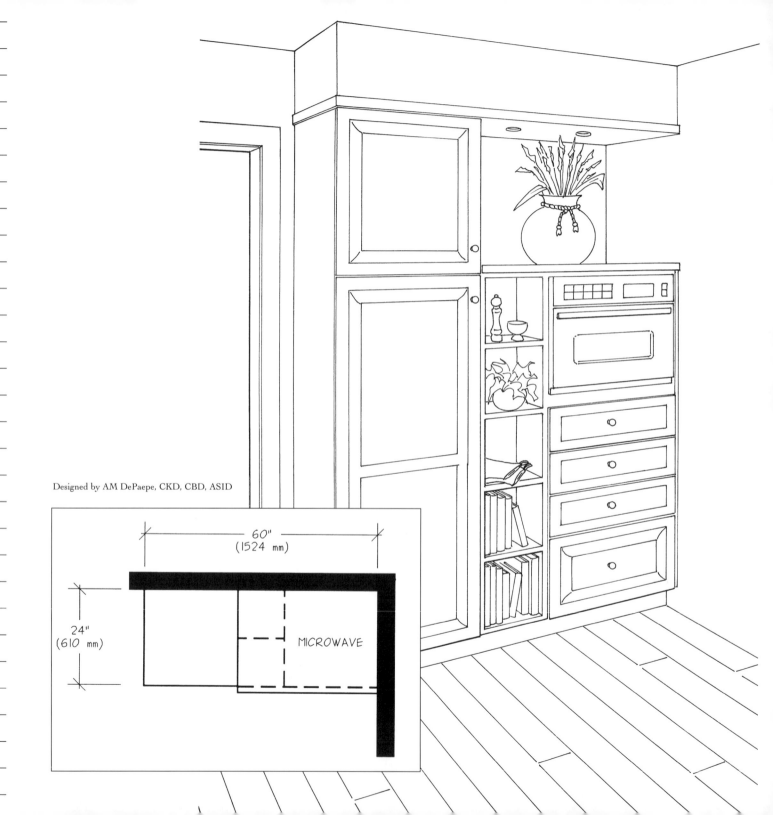

Designed by AM DePaepe, CKD, CBD, ASID

48"
(1219 mm)

66"
(1676 mm)

OVEN

Designed by AM DePaepe,
CKD, CBD, ASID
Plan drawn to 1/4" scale

The visual impact of this diagonal installation is enhanced by extending the cabinet up to the 8' ceiling. An arched opening at the top of the unit calls attention to this detail. The 27"-wide oven cabinet is flanked by 3"-wide tall fillers that make 135-degree angles with their return panels. The angled unit occupies 42" of wall space out of the corner in each direction. On either side of the oven cabinet are 6"-wide, angled-front base units left open to hold baking sheets and serving trays. To the right, an 18"-wide base provides both storage and landing space.

Design Note: Recessing the cabinet further into the corner and/or reducing the filler size will lessen the amount of total space taken up by the corner unit. However, installing it as shown here will provide more flexibility on the job site.

Continuing the arched valance detailing from adjacent cabinets onto this microwave center makes it an integral aspect of the overall cabinet design. The 36"-wide microwave cabinet is centered between 36"-wide x 60"-high wall cabinet/appliance garage combination units. Since the microwave is only 24" wide, the extra space on each side is used to hold frequently-used cookbooks. Like the wall cabinets, each of the three base cabinets is 36" wide. The three-drawer bank in the central base exaggerates the break in design detail above.

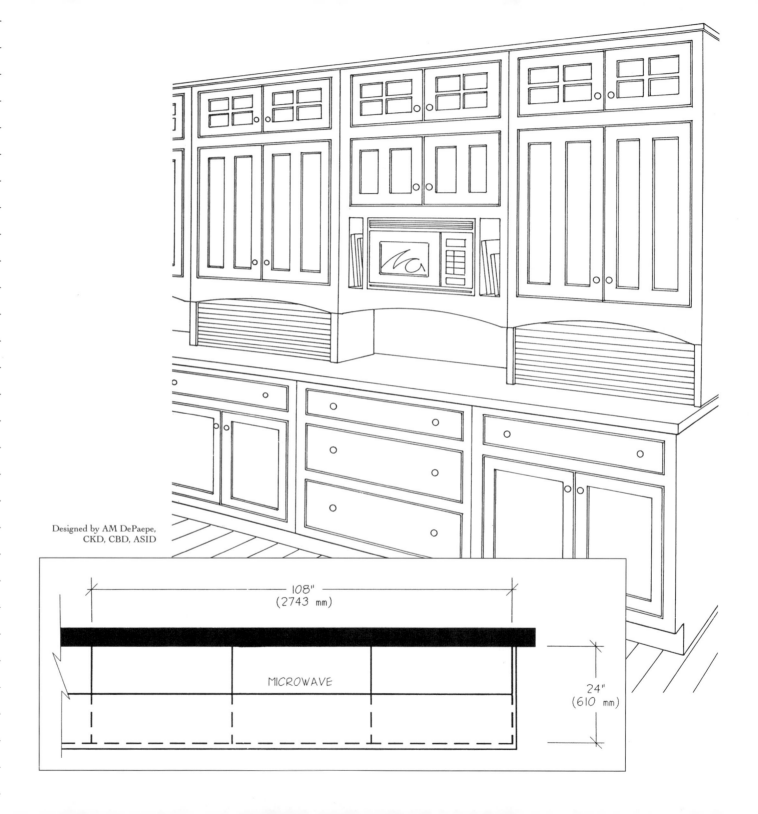

Designed by AM DePaepe,
CKD, CBD, ASID

108"
(2743 mm)

MICROWAVE

24"
(610 mm)

Designed by AM DePaepe,
CKD, CBD, ASID

84"
(2134 mm)

MICROWAVE

27"
(686 mm)

Traditional details and modern convenience combine to create this stand-alone bake center. The area is framed on two sides by 6"-wide x 27"-deep pilasters. The corbels at their tops seem to hold up the extended soffit. The 36"-wide base cabinets house two 30"-wide single ovens. The wall cabinet, which measures 36" wide x 18" deep x 48" high, features a drawer at the bottom and an open arch at the top. On the right side, two pot/ utensil racks span across the the wall area. The 6"-deep shelf below is made from a 36" length of corbel molding that matches the pilaster details. A built-in hot plate is made by routing a solid surface counter and inserting steel rods to hold dishes off its surface.

This microwave and second sink location is designed for children to use for snacks and craft projects. The 21"-wide x 10"-high microwave is located under a 36"-high countertop. A 3" filler and 24"-deep return panels support both the microwave shelf and the 21"-high pullout counter just below. An open area below the counter easily stores two pint-sized stools. To the left of the microwave are 30"-wide open shelves and a drawer box on casters. The glass doors in the 25"-wide wall cabinet create a tidy display space for art projects. Lowered to 30" high, the adjacent counter has 34" of open knee area—perfect for an older child to sit. A sink is within easy reach for cleanup. As children grow, the shelves and toy box can be removed to create a kitchen work station.

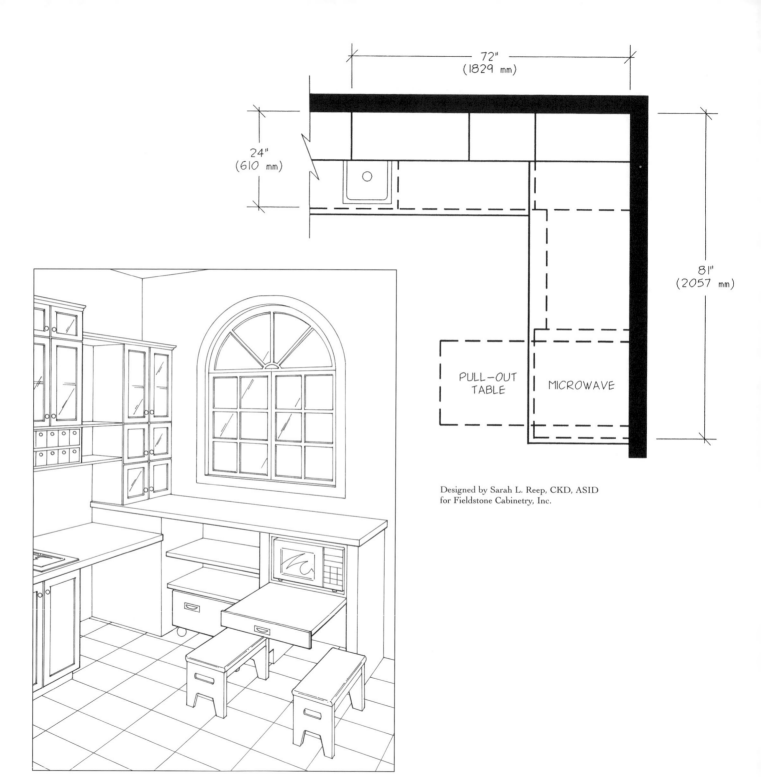

Designed by Sarah L. Reep, CKD, ASID
for Fieldstone Cabinetry, Inc.

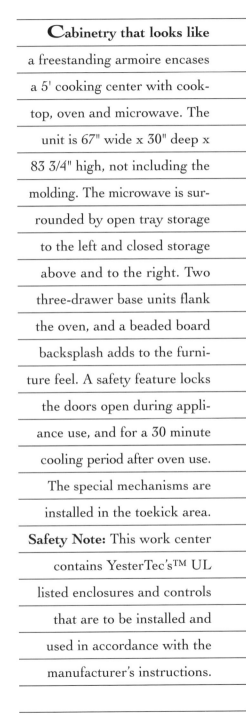

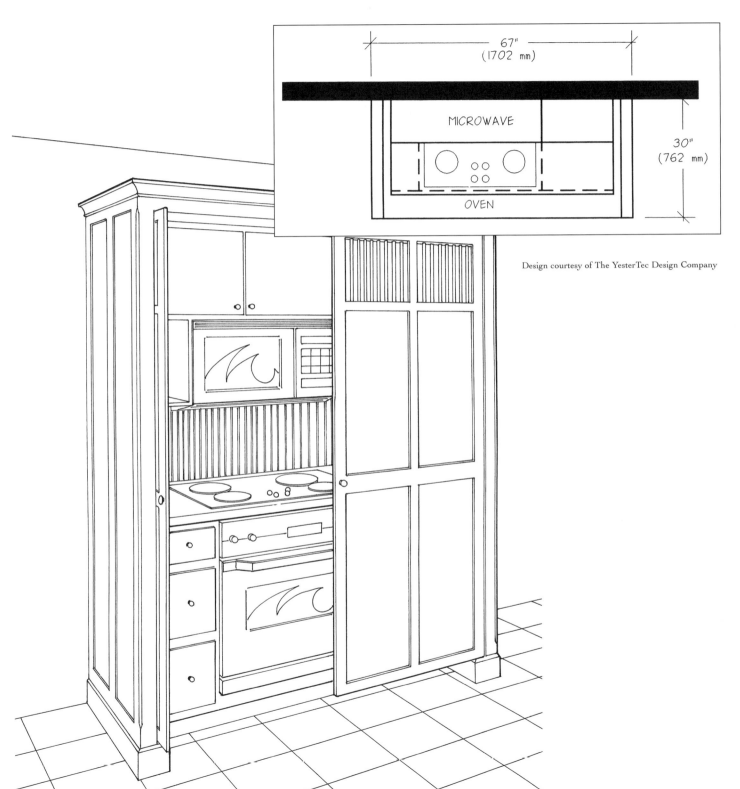

67"
(1702 mm)

MICROWAVE

OVEN

30"
(762 mm)

Design courtesy of The YesterTec Design Company

Cabinetry that looks like a freestanding armoire encases a 5' cooking center with cooktop, oven and microwave. The unit is 67" wide x 30" deep x 83 3/4" high, not including the molding. The microwave is surrounded by open tray storage to the left and closed storage above and to the right. Two three-drawer base units flank the oven, and a beaded board backsplash adds to the furniture feel. A safety feature locks the doors open during appliance use, and for a 30 minute cooling period after oven use. The special mechanisms are installed in the toekick area.

Safety Note: This work center contains YesterTec's™ UL listed enclosures and controls that are to be installed and used in accordance with the manufacturer's instructions.

A traditional piece of furniture reminiscent of a pie safe is what you see when these cabinet doors are closed. But opened up they reveal a double oven cabinet with two drawers at the bottom. The unit's over-all dimensions are 43" wide x 30" deep x 75" high, including the molding. A special safety feature locks the flipper doors in the open position during oven use, as well as for 30 minutes after use for cooling. Special installation mechanisms are installed in the toekick area of the cabinet.

Safety Note: The oven enclosure illustrated on this page contains YesterTec's™ UL listed enclosures and controls that are to be installed and used in accordance with the manufacturer's instructions.

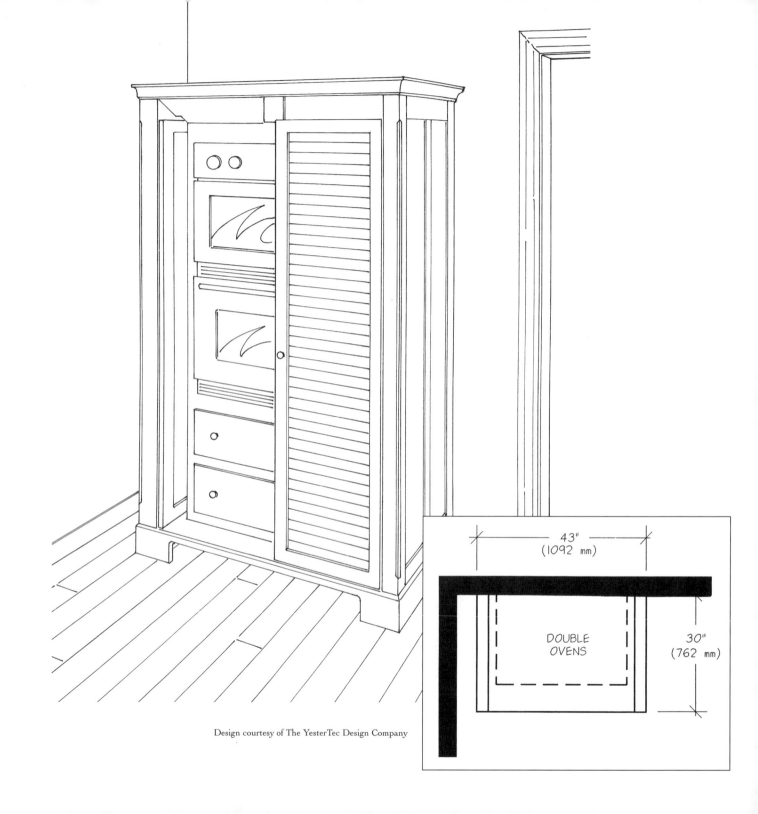

43"
(1092 mm)

DOUBLE
OVENS

30"
(762 mm)

Design courtesy of The YesterTec Design Company

Design by Nick Geragi, CKD, CBD, ASID

DOUBLE
OVENS

54"
(1372 mm)

MICROWAVE

24"
(610 mm)

48"
(1219 mm)

People will stop to look at this bake center that forms a partial octagon. The 30"-wide x 84"-high double oven cabinet is of standard configuration. To begin the octagonal shape, an angled 12"-wide x 24"-deep front cabinet is set with its back against the oven cabinet. Proceeding in the same direction, the next cabinet is 24" wide with four drawers. Another angled base on the opposite side completes the design. A 24"-wide microwave cabinet extends to the ceiling and features an open shelf with a valance at its top. Reflecting the angles of the base cabinets are 12"-wide x 30"-high diagonal open shelf units.

CHAPTER FIVE

Specialty Centers

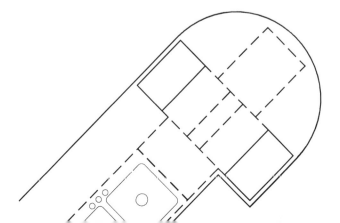

This kitchen peninsula terminates with a snack center built for two. While the area is integral with the rest of the kitchen, its two columnar structures set it off, suggesting a separate function. This also protects the cook's primary work centers from intruders. The columns are created by extending wall cabinets down to the counter, surrounding them with paneling and extending facia moldings to the ceiling. The 36"-high counter-top is extended from the sink center to form the snack sur-face. An 18"-wide, central wine rack defines two knee areas. This design feature encourages socialization by allowing users to face one another.

Designed by Sarah L. Reep, CKD, ASID for
Fieldstone Cabinetry, Inc.

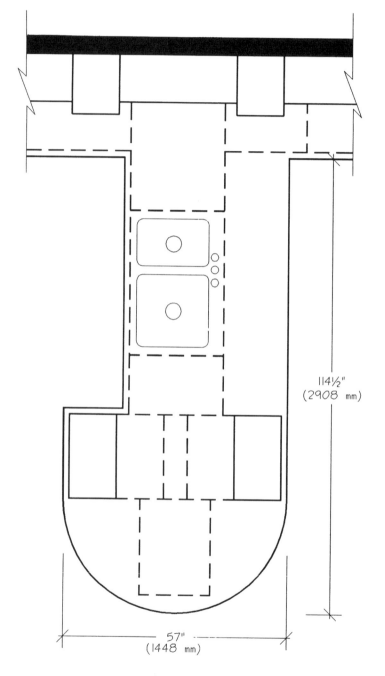

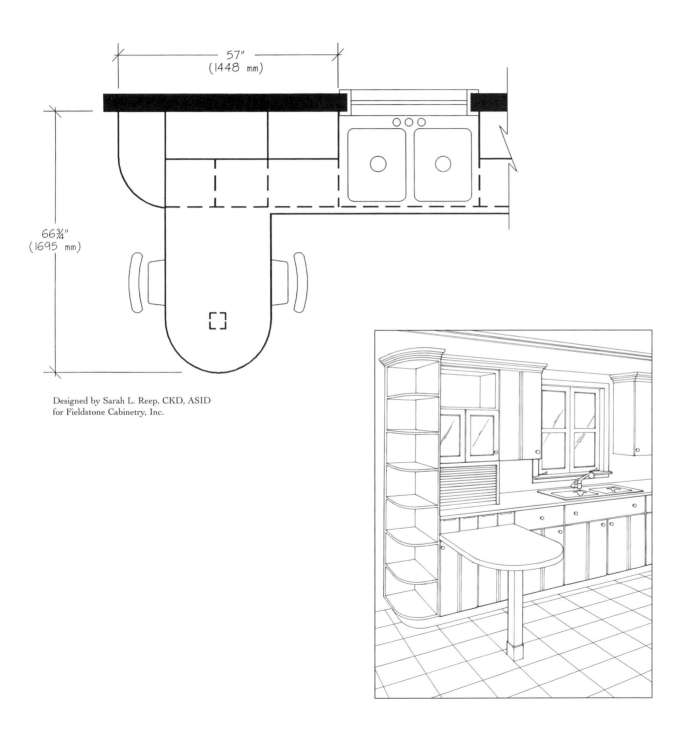

57"
(1448 mm)

66¾"
(1695 mm)

Designed by Sarah L. Reep, CKD, ASID
for Fieldstone Cabinetry, Inc.

The end of a wall of cabinets is the perfect site for a small snack center. This one, adjacent to the primary sink center, doubles as a seated work station. The wall cabinets directly behind the table extend to the counter to increase access to storage. A 27"-wide appliance garage and a row of 4 1/2"-high apothecary drawers handily hold snack foods and utensils. More difficult to reach, the top part of the wall cabinet is designated for display. Below the table, a 28 1/2"-high base cabinet provides closed storage for infrequently-used items. The table top extends 42 3/4" out from the base cabinets and ends in a half circle. It is supported by a 4"-square post with a 4"-high baseboard. A 12"-wide x 24"-deep x 84"-high whatnot shelf repeats the table's curvilinear detail.

An eat-in kitchen is easy to plan if you build the table into the cabinetry. In this design, a 60" table is sandwiched between two tall cabinets, which each measure 30" wide x 24" deep x 96" tall. The table, traditional in detail, is 30" high and extends 51" from the wall. It rests on a 9"-square column. Two 18"-wide x 48"-high wall cabinets featuring mullioned glass doors and two drawers flank a 24"-wide x 30"-high cabinet, also equipped with mullioned glass doors. The void at the center back portion of the tabletop can be used to display personal treasures, or to house condiments.

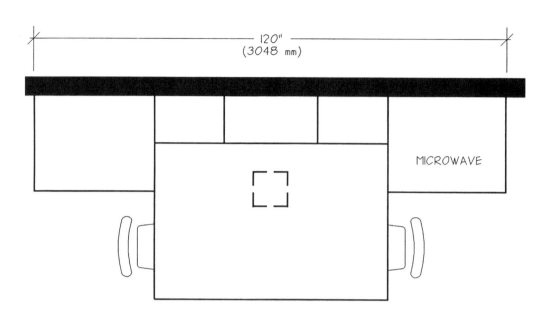

120"
(3048 mm)

MICROWAVE

Designed by
Alan Asarnow, CKD, CBD, CR

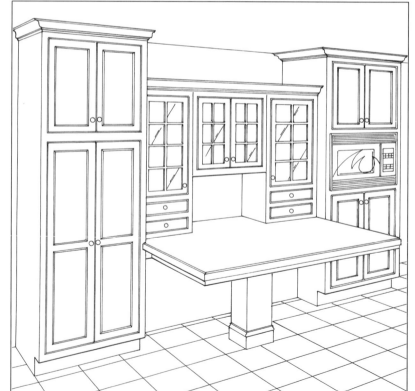

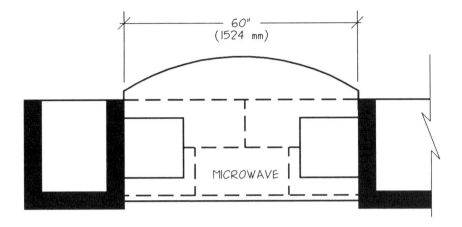

60"
(1524 mm)

MICROWAVE

Designed by AM DePaepe,
CKD, CBD, ASID

Removing a 60"-wide x
72"-high section of wall and
built-in shelving from an adjacent family room made way for
this large pass-through, which
features closed storage, double-
sided display and a snack bar.
On the kitchen side (shown),
the 12"-deep x 28 1/2"-high
base cabinets include four
doors, two open shelves and a
small microwave. The two wall
cabinets above, measuring 15"
wide x 15" deep x 48" high,
have two glass doors/panels on
their three exposed sides, and
are accessible from both the
kitchen and the family room.
On the family room side of the
unit a countertop snack bar
gently curves into the room,
maximizing seating capacity.

A small breakfast nook for two includes a view without forsaking storage needs. A long, 12"-deep wall of storage is punctured by a 72" x 36" window-and-countertop expanse. The cantilevered breakfast table extends out from the wall's midsection, forming a half circle. It is flanked by two tall cabinets, each measuring 30" wide x 90" high. The 36"-wide x 24"-high wall cabinets above the window align with the doors on the adjacent tall cabinets. Two 18"-wide x 28 1/2"-high base cabinets help to support the counter; they also help to create a frame for the central fluted column support.

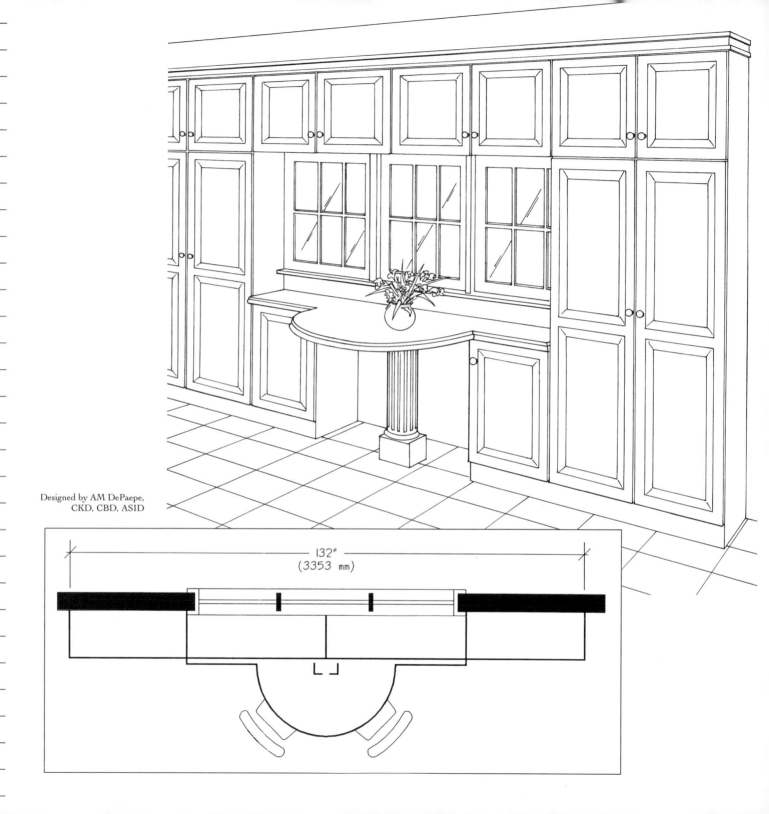

Designed by AM DePaepe,
CKD, CBD, ASID

132"
(3353 mm)

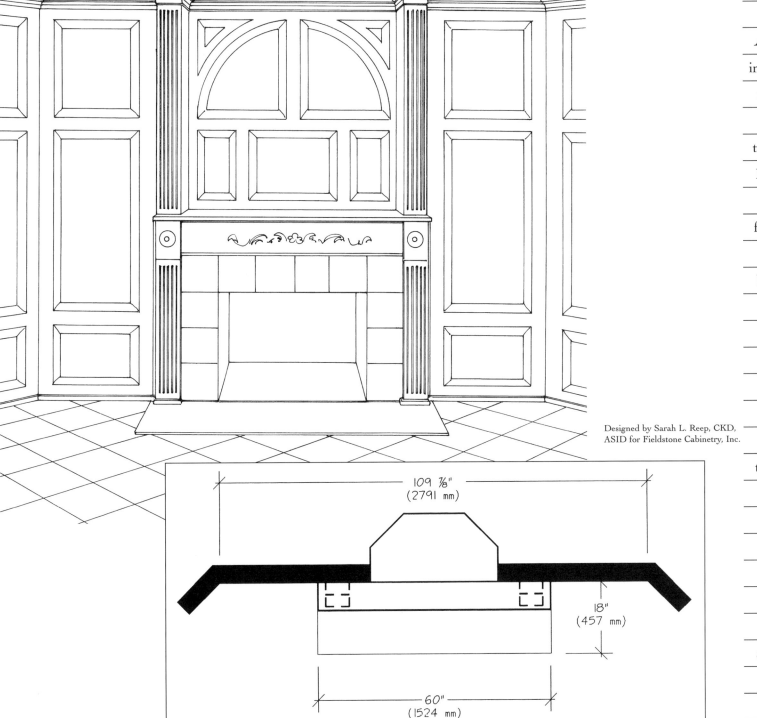

Designed by Sarah L. Reep, CKD,
ASID for Fieldstone Cabinetry, Inc.

109 ⅞"
(2791 mm)

18"
(457 mm)

60"
(1524 mm)

A **fireplace is right at home**
in today's kitchen as consumers
finally acknowledge this room
as the most comfortable place
to entertain family and friends.
Here, a 60"-wide fireplace in a
paneled wall is set apart by
floor-to-ceiling fluted columns,
creating an extraordinary
backdrop for any social gather-
ing. The fireplace opening
is defined by a border of
12"-square tiles. Two 6"-wide
fluted panels and an 8"-high
valance board adorned with
an onlay surround the row of
tiles. These moldings are bound
by two 10"-high x 6"-wide
corner blocks. Two 3/4"-thick
pieces of solid stone are used
for the hearth and mantel.
Decorative panel moldings
above the mantel and on
adjacent wall surfaces complete
the architectural focal point.

Traditionally referred to as wet bars, areas like this one really serve as much more in contemporary households. This one is used as a beverage center to serve family members of all ages, as well as for myriad other functions. The base includes an 18"-wide ice maker, a 30"-wide sink base with angled fillers and a 24"-wide beverage/wine chiller. Wall cabinets include two 24"-wide x 48"-high units; these rest on the countertop, providing varied storage both in and out of reach of younger users. The 36"-wide x 24"-high center wall cabinet with mullioned glass doors has a rack mounted to its bottom for hanging stemware.

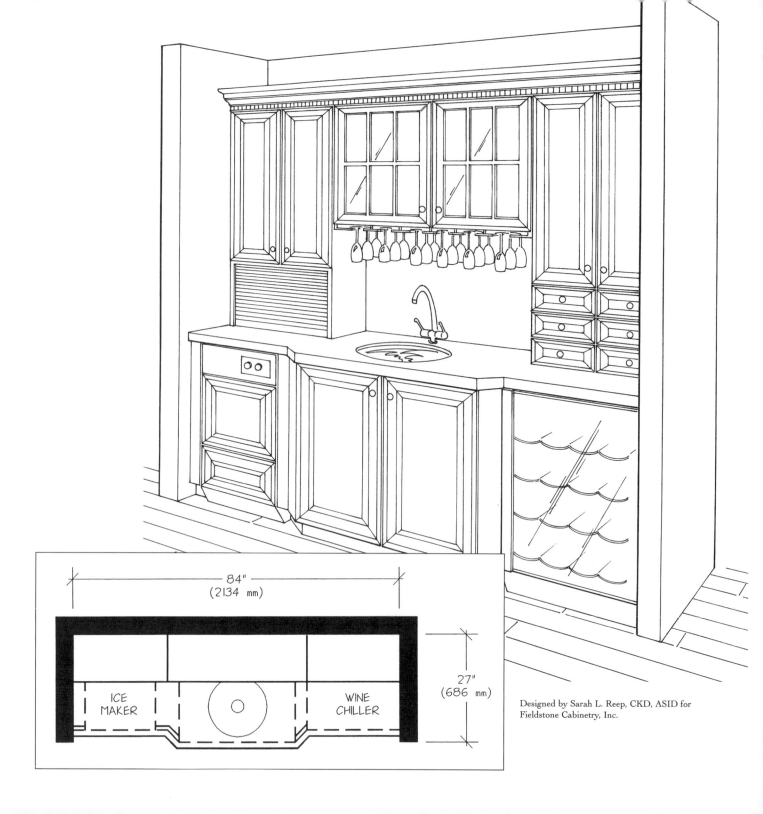

84"
(2134 mm)

27"
(686 mm)

ICE MAKER

WINE CHILLER

Designed by Sarah L. Reep, CKD, ASID for Fieldstone Cabinetry, Inc.

Designed by Plain & Fancy Custom Cabinetry

84"
(2134 mm)

24"
(610 mm)

Since families are spending more leisure time at home than ever before, hobby centers are back in full force—and one of the most popular hobbies today is gardening. This potting center has everything a hobby gardener needs: a view of the garden, open shelving for easy access to books and tools, a large utility sink and peg storage. Its 84"-long run of cabinets consists of a 24"-wide base, a 30"-wide sink base and a 30"-wide double door base. The large doors accommodate oversized pots, bags of dirt and various tools. The open wall cabinet, measuring 30" wide x 31 1/2" high, provides an asymmetrical balance to the off-center window with extended sill.

Located along an 84"-long return wall that terminates at the main kitchen area, this potting center shares its sink with the cook's helper. The 18"-wide drawer base to the right of the sink may serve either user; the official separation point is the 60"-high wall cabinet with mullioned glass door and 24"-wide appliance garage. To this cabinet's right, wall cabinets are hung 84" above the floor, leaving an open soffit to display plants and accessories. Centered between 15"-wide wall cabinets, a 30"-wide x 30"-high open shelf unit features built-in plant lights behind light valances. Base cabinets include a 42"-wide blind cabinet; a 21"-wide closed unit; and a 21"-wide unit with pullout baskets. The baskets can be easily removed and carried out to the garden.

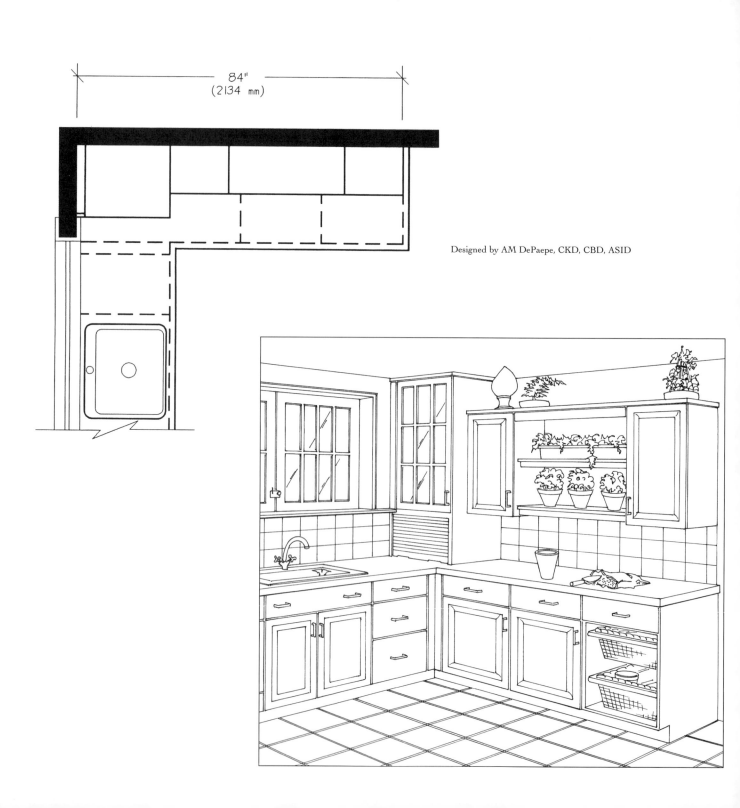

84"
(2134 mm)

Designed by AM DePaepe, CKD, CBD, ASID

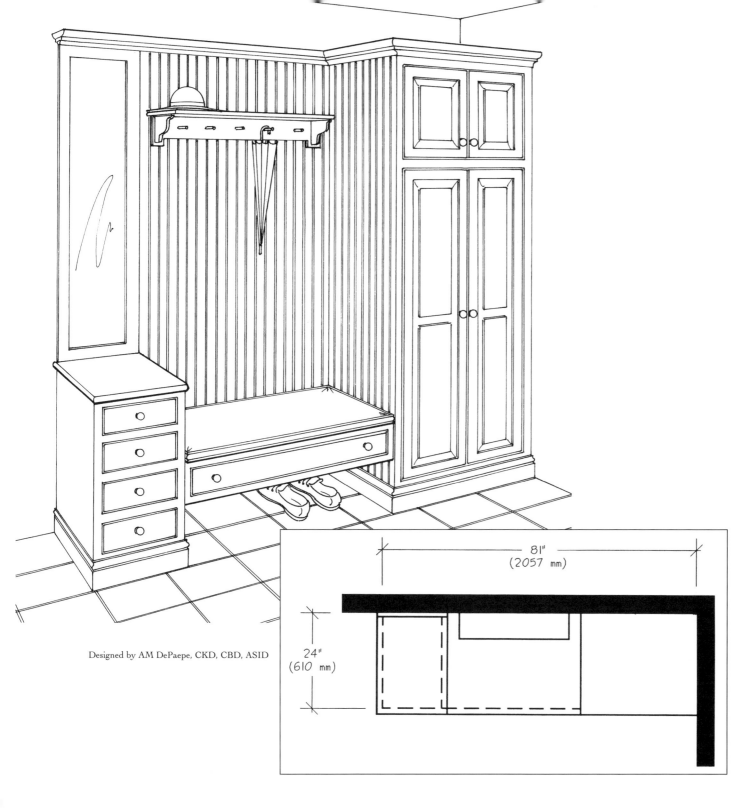

Designed by AM DePaepe, CKD, CBD, ASID

81"
(2057 mm)

24"
(610 mm)

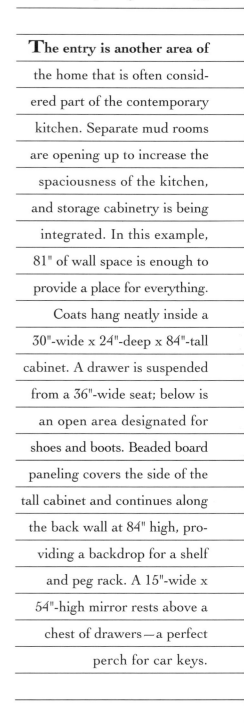

The entry is another area of the home that is often considered part of the contemporary kitchen. Separate mud rooms are opening up to increase the spaciousness of the kitchen, and storage cabinetry is being integrated. In this example, 81" of wall space is enough to provide a place for everything. Coats hang neatly inside a 30"-wide x 24"-deep x 84"-tall cabinet. A drawer is suspended from a 36"-wide seat; below is an open area designated for shoes and boots. Beaded board paneling covers the side of the tall cabinet and continues along the back wall at 84" high, providing a backdrop for a shelf and peg rack. A 15"-wide x 54"-high mirror rests above a chest of drawers—a perfect perch for car keys.

This 82 1/2"-wide storage center is a more formal approach to an entry area. The 21"-wide x 18"-deep tall cabinet is 72" high and features pullout hooks for easy coat storage. Shoes are housed inside the tall unit on two low shelves, which can be removed for cleaning. The 60"-wide seat doubles as a place to rest purses, briefcases and backpacks. Two 30"-wide x 18"-deep drawers provide storage for the same. A large mirror and frame measures 60" wide x 54" high.

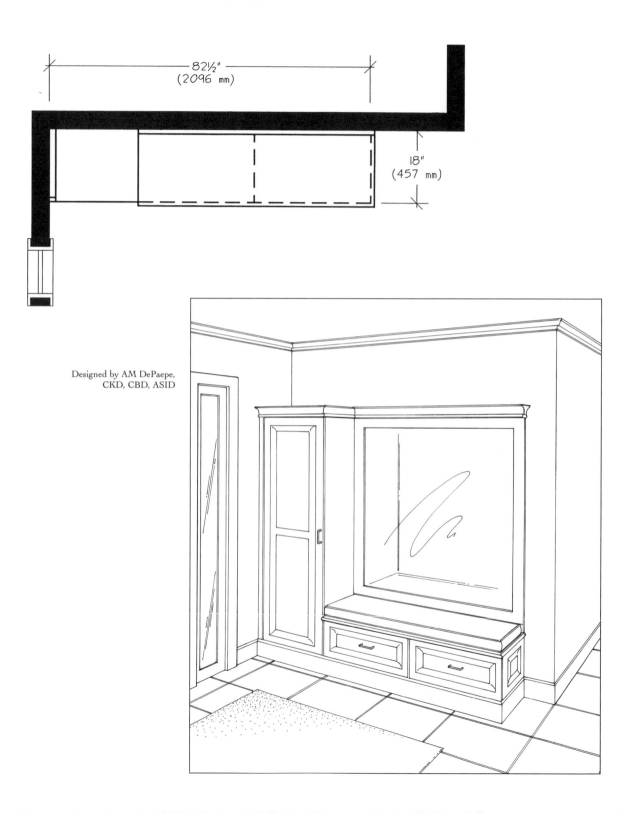

Designed by AM DePaepe,
CKD, CBD, ASID

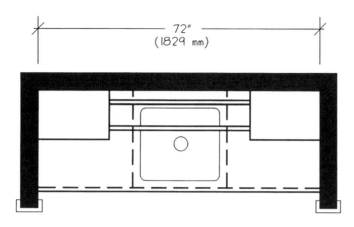

72"
(1829 mm)

Designed by AM DePaepe, CKD, CBD, ASID

Often integrated into the kitchen, the laundry center is another specialized area that merits efficient, organized storage. This one might replace a walk-through mud room. The utility sink is housed in the center of three 24"-wide base cabinets. Two 18"-wide x 30"-high open wall cabinets anchor two laundry poles, allowing users space to hang clothing over the sink. The opposite wall (not shown) accommodates the washer, dryer and utility shelves.

This laundry center encloses a stacked washer/dryer in its own room, allowing the unit to be hidden behind doors when it is not in use. To its right, the last 52 1/2" of kitchen cabinets are dedicated to the laundry center. A 36"-wide base includes a small sink at the left to accommodate hand washables. A 36"-wide x 12"-high wall cabinet is installed high above the sink, leaving plenty of space to hang laundry from the pole. The 15"-wide x 24"-deep tall cabinet opens to reveal a fold-down ironing board and storage.

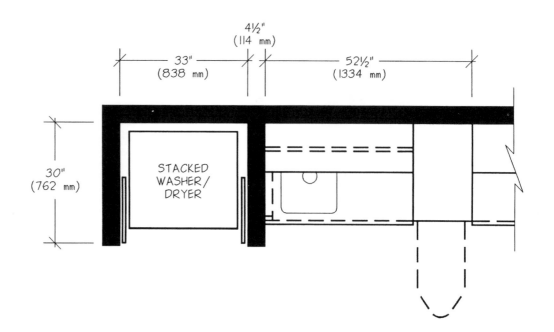

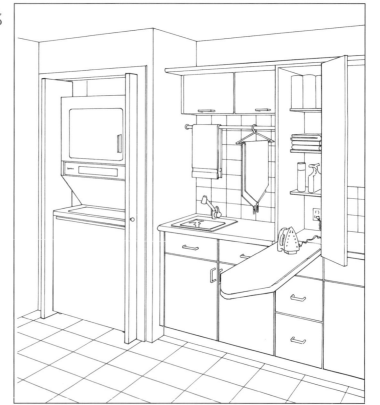

Designed by AM DePaepe,
CKD, CBD, ASID

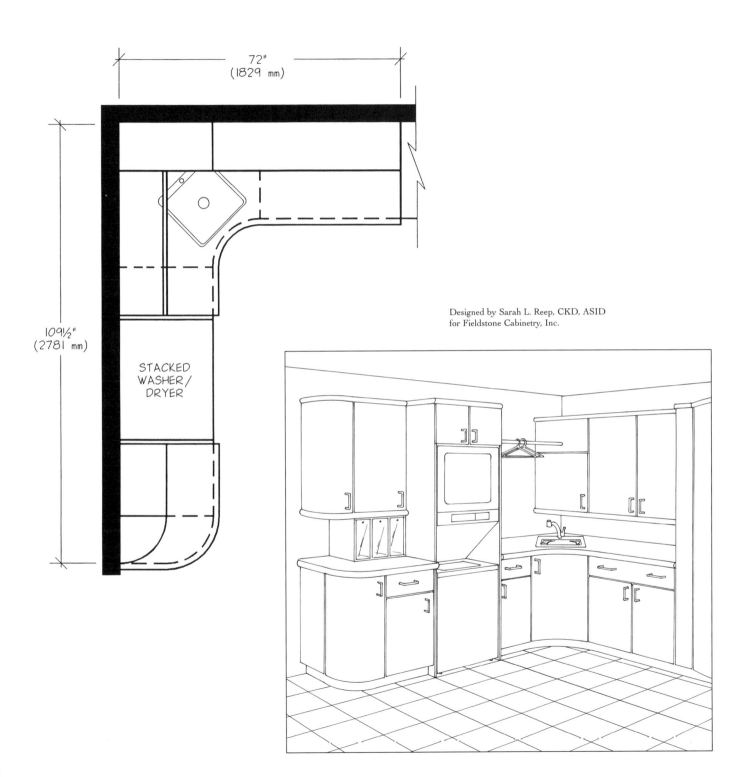

72"
(1829 mm)

109½"
(2781 mm)

STACKED
WASHER/
DRYER

Designed by Sarah L. Reep, CKD, ASID
for Fieldstone Cabinetry, Inc.

This large laundry center occupies 55 sq. ft. of floor space. It starts with 12"-wide, curved end cabinets for both wall and base. These are followed by two 18"-wide units. Three plexiglass bins at the backsplash hold detergents; the base unit has a pullout ironing board in its drawer. Next, a stacked washer/dryer unit fits snugly between two tall end panels. A 12"-high wall cabinet sits on top. To the right, base storage includes a 12"-wide cabinet, a 36"-wide corner sink cabinet and a 36"-wide cabinet. Above, a laundry pole is suspended between the washer/dryer and the cabinet in the corner, which is 24" wide x 30" high and has an 18"-high working door. The remaining wall cabinet measures 42" wide x 30" high.

A small sandwich-making area and single-person snack counter become points of interest in this kitchen design. The area is accented by protruding the 36"-wide base cabinet 3" in front of the others. Above, end panels extend to the counter, framing a 24"-high wall cabinet and open shelves. Extra-tall, 48"-high x 18"-wide wall cabinets are hung on either side of the end panels. To the left, the wall angles 135 degrees, providing an interesting junction for the curvilinear snack counter. Set just under a window, the counter is a wonderful place to sip a cup of coffee or enjoy a midday meal.

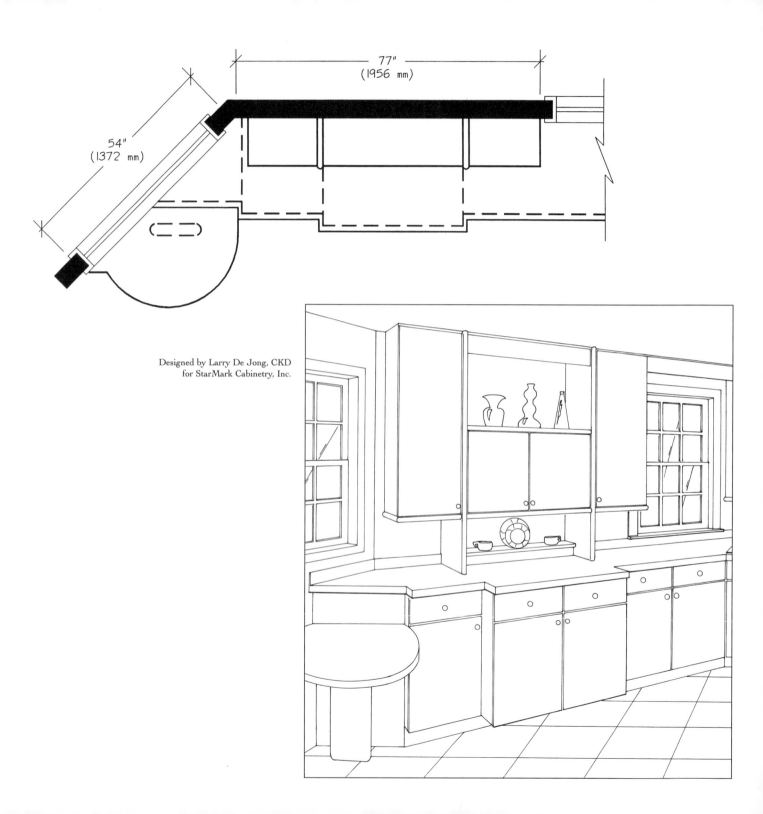

Designed by Larry De Jong, CKD
for StarMark Cabinetry, Inc.

CHAPTER SIX

Display Centers

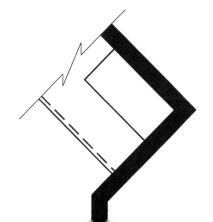

This display center is a freestanding hutch of heirloom quality. The details begin at the base, which is made up of two cabinets—one 21" and the other 42" wide. These cabinets, which feature a 3/4"-thick shelf edge molding at their bottom, sit atop four ball feet in lieu of a toekick. The hutch top is custom made as a single piece, which is seemingly supported by wood brackets that measure 12" x 12" x 4". Across the unit's 24"-high, 63"-wide mid-section are three mullioned glass doors. Above the doors, an open shelf is adorned with a triple arched valance board and four flattened spindle-shaped supports. A 3" crown molding finishes off the top, helping the unit to reach its 87" overall height.

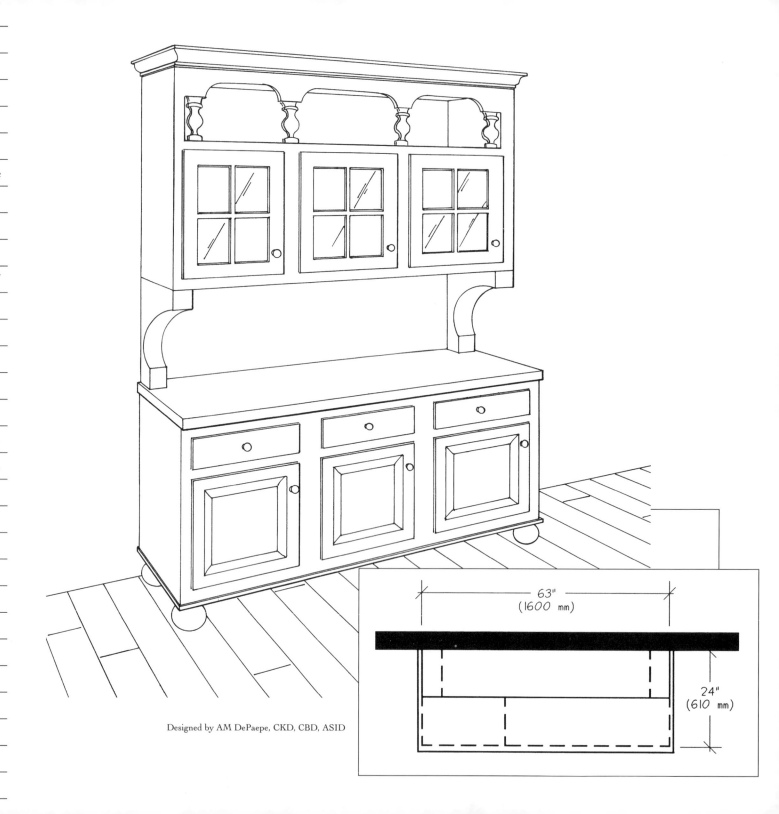

Designed by AM DePaepe, CKD, CBD, ASID

63"
(1600 mm)

24"
(610 mm)

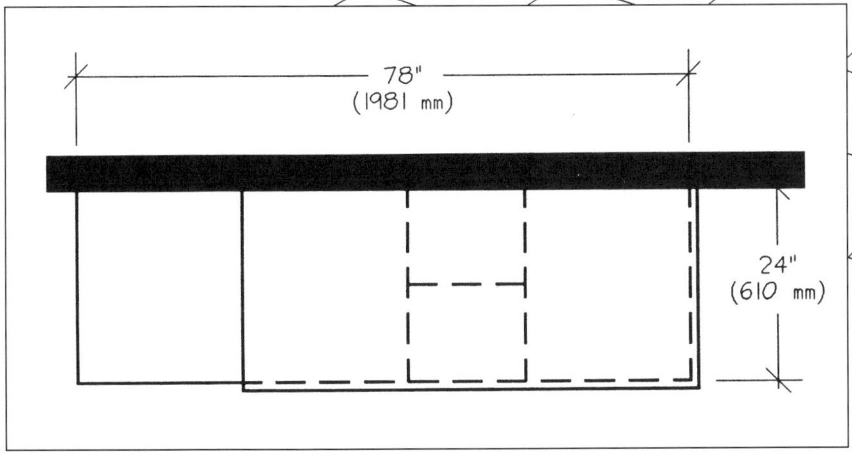

Simply dropping the height of two tall cabinets and separating them with suspended shelves creates a unique display center in a wall of storage. On the left is a standard 21"-wide x 84"-high tall cabinet; the shorter two cabinets are 21" wide x 60" high. The 15" gap between the two cabinets is filled with three shelves. A back panel provides these shelves with a boundary. A 3/4" counter caps this area, creating an open display that measures 57" wide x 24" deep.

78"
(1981 mm)

24"
(610 mm)

Designed by AM DePaepe, CKD, CBD, ASID

Since it generally faces a table area, the back side of an island is a natural place to display dishes and a wine collection. The glass-doored center cabinet on the back of this island has 36"-wide x 12"-deep shelves to show off dishware; its 42"-high countertop hides the cooktop from diners' view. The 18"-wide x 12"-deep x 34 1/2"-high cabinets with wine racks also extend the cooktop's work surface. Shaping the counter edge profile like a cove molding establishes a free-standing furniture feel.

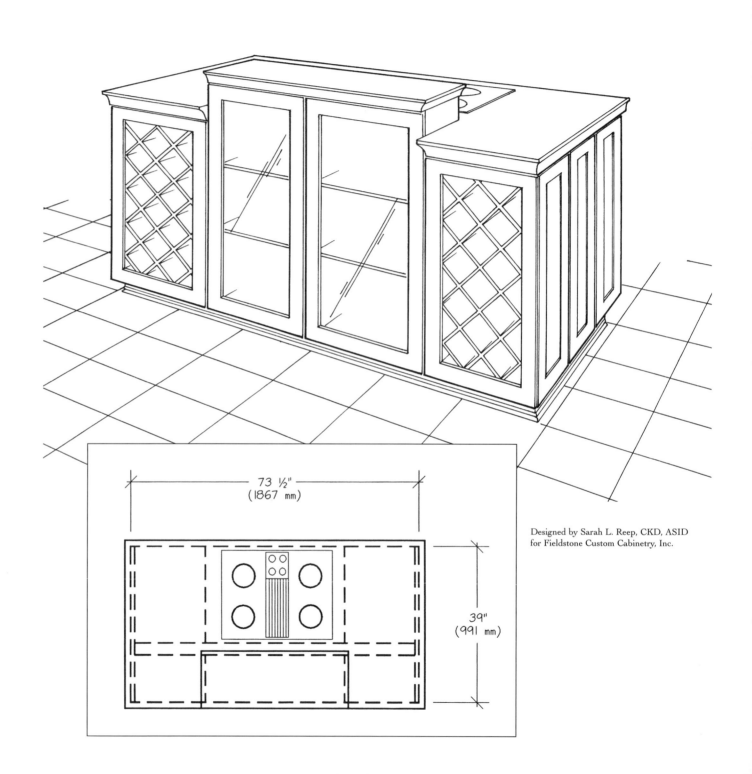

73 ½"
(1867 mm)

39"
(991 mm)

Designed by Sarah L. Reep, CKD, ASID
for Fieldstone Custom Cabinetry, Inc.

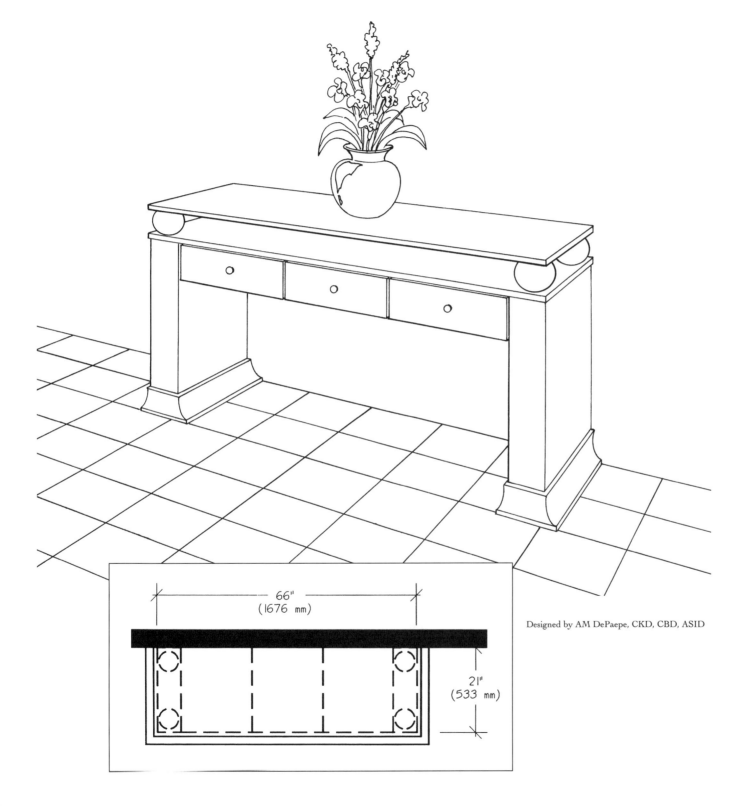

Designed by AM DePaepe, CKD, CBD, ASID

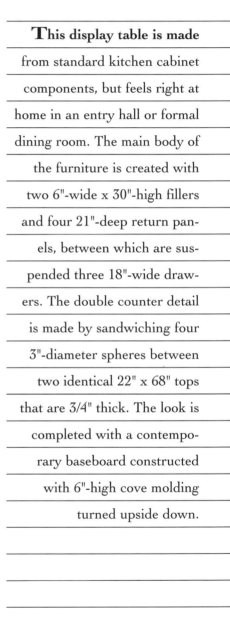

This display table is made from standard kitchen cabinet components, but feels right at home in an entry hall or formal dining room. The main body of the furniture is created with two 6"-wide x 30"-high fillers and four 21"-deep return panels, between which are suspended three 18"-wide drawers. The double counter detail is made by sandwiching four 3"-diameter spheres between two identical 22" x 68" tops that are 3/4" thick. The look is completed with a contemporary baseboard constructed with 6"-high cove molding turned upside down.

Since kitchen space is often open to other areas of the home, cabinetry can be called upon to serve multiple purposes. This unit efficiently includes closed storage, closed and open display space and a shelf specifically designated for a television. The center cabinet is 42" wide and is comprised of a 15"-high x 24"-deep base with a protruding TV shelf; the opening for the TV is 24" high. The split doors of the 18"-wide x 60"-high tall cabinets at each side align with the 15"-high center base cabinet doors. Atop all three cabinets are diagonal end components that are turned on their sides to form triangular open shelves. These shelves measure 24" deep x 12" high.

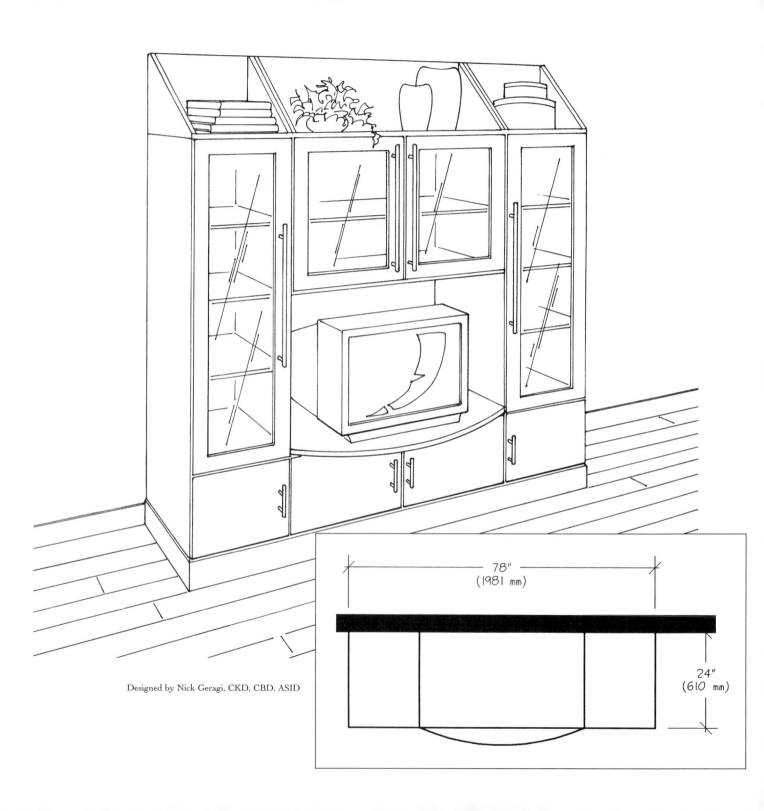

Designed by Nick Geragi, CKD, CBD, ASID

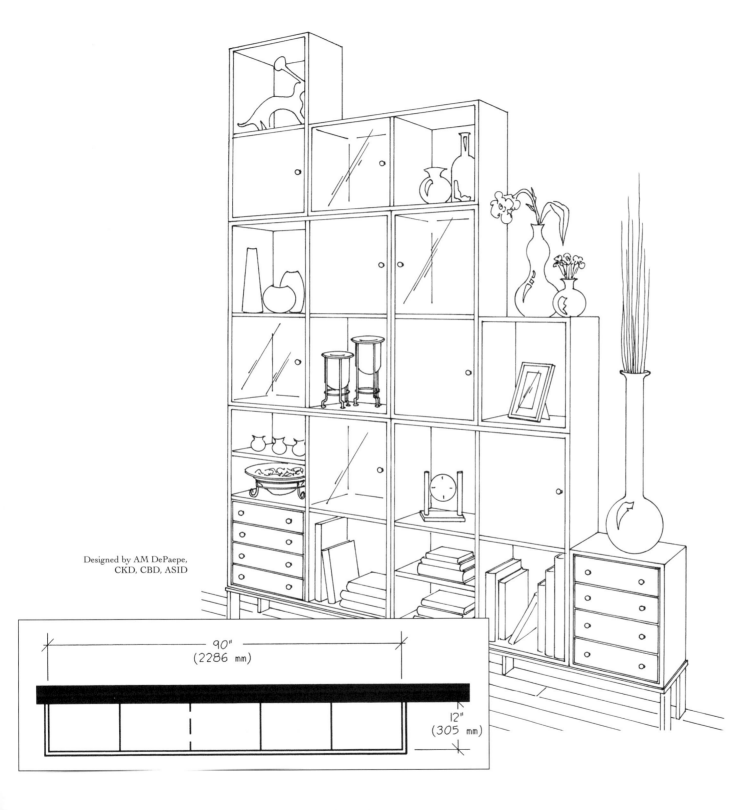

Designed by AM DePaepe,
CKD, CBD, ASID

90"
(2286 mm)

12"
(305 mm)

Taking a cue from a room's vaulted ceiling, this tiered display center is comprised of cubes stacked up like building blocks. The cubes, which each measure 18" wide x 18" high x 12" deep, sit on a set of three base supports. Each support consists of four legs and a 3/4" shelf. The outside supports are each 36" wide; the center support is 18" wide. This symmetry, coupled with the two four-drawer inserts at each end of the bottom row, anchors the otherwise asymmetrical design. The remaining cubes display an interesting mix of solid doors, glass doors and open storage. The four solid doors diagonally climb the unit, emphasizing the angled ceiling.

Elegant details make this traditionally-styled display hutch the perfect place to showcase fine china and family collectibles. Eight turned pilasters set the design theme; along the outside of the unit, these pilasters are mounted onto 3"-wide extended stiles. The two 18"-wide x 48"-high wall cabinets extend to the countertop, helping to frame the open shelves at their center. An 18"-wide base with open pullout baskets is flanked by two 9"-wide open tray bases and two 18"-wide base cabinets. The entire unit is set on a flush toekick and baseboard molding. The molding features three flat arch shapes that align perfectly with the pilasters.

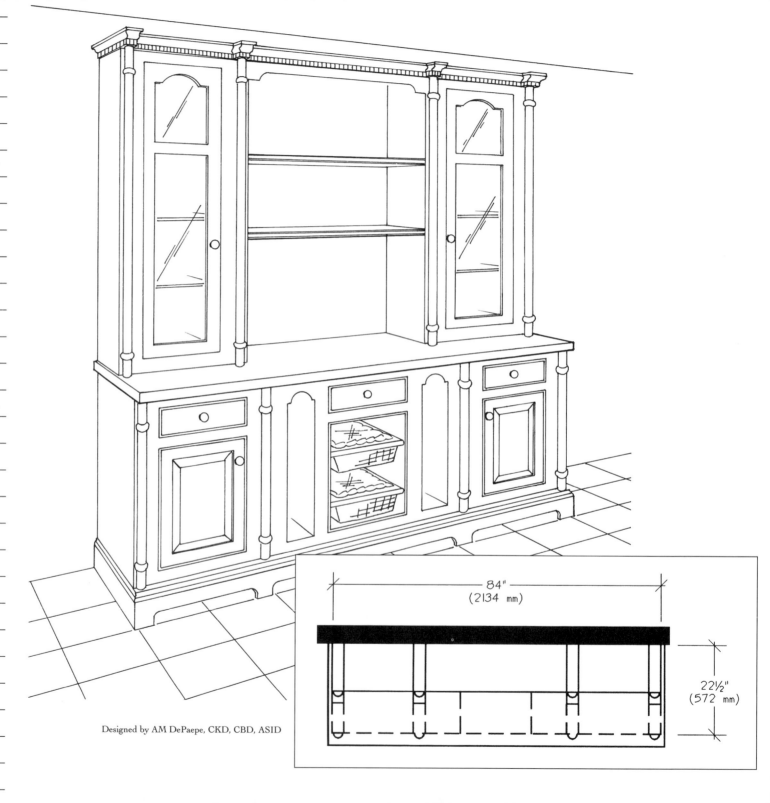

Designed by AM DePaepe, CKD, CBD, ASID

84"
(2134 mm)

22½"
(572 mm)

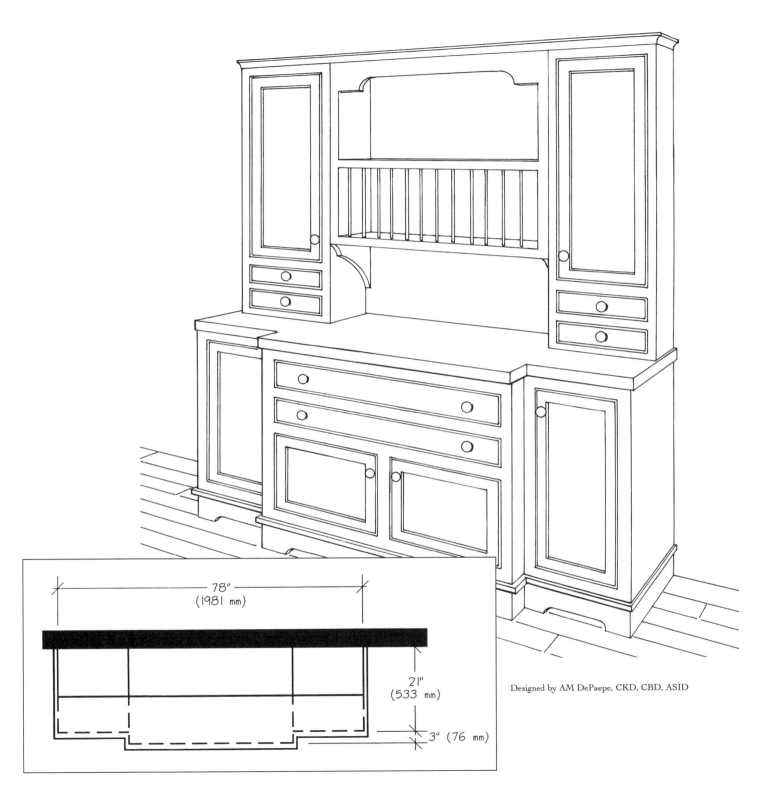

Designed by AM DePaepe, CKD, CBD, ASID

78"
(1981 mm)

21"
(533 mm)

3" (76 mm)

The simple shaker details of this hutch will place all of the attention on the clients' possessions. Two 18"-wide x 48"-high wall cabinets frame the central display area, which is 42" wide x 36" high. The center wall cabinet, which rests on 8"-high brackets, features a 21"-high open shelf and valance and a 15"-high plate rack. The end base cabinets are 18" wide, 21" deep and 34 1/2" high. The 42"-wide center base is pulled forward 3", resulting in a 24" depth. Three flat arch valances replace toekicks. The hutch is completed with a small cove molding at its top.

An open soffit is a natural place to display collectibles in a small traditional-style kitchen—but remember that the display area does not have to stop where the cabinets end. Stretching the display area over a doorway by cantilevering a 13"-deep shelf connects cabinetry and brings continuity to the space. The shelf and its display objects make an interesting focal point over the door opening. This concept can also be applied to designs with cabinets that extend to the ceiling by butting the shelf above the door to the sides of adjacent cabinets. In either situation, it is important to make sure that the wall reveals between the cabinet ends and the door casing or opening are equal.

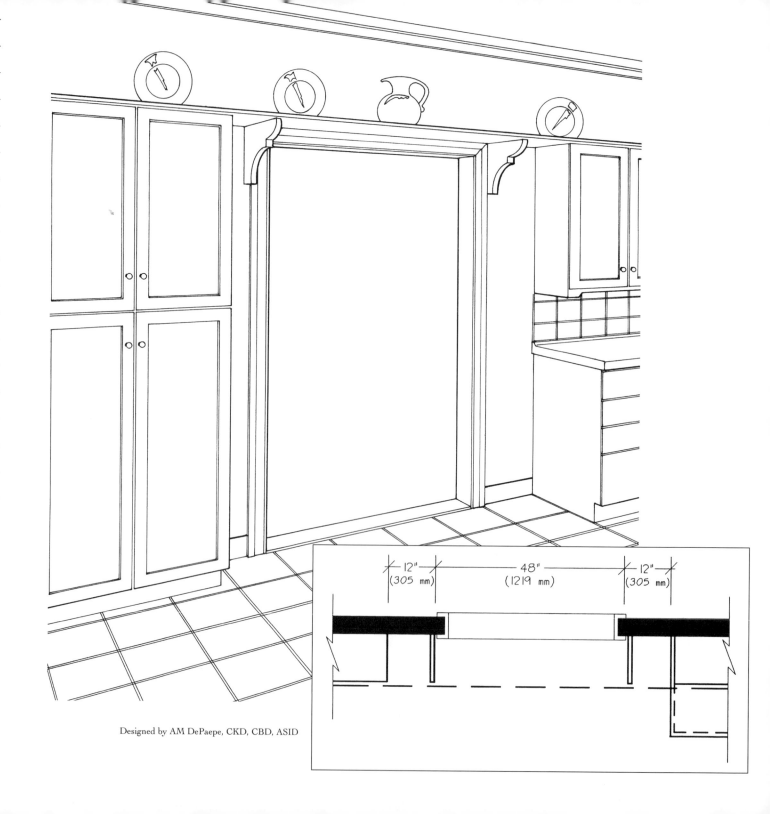

Designed by AM DePaepe, CKD, CBD, ASID

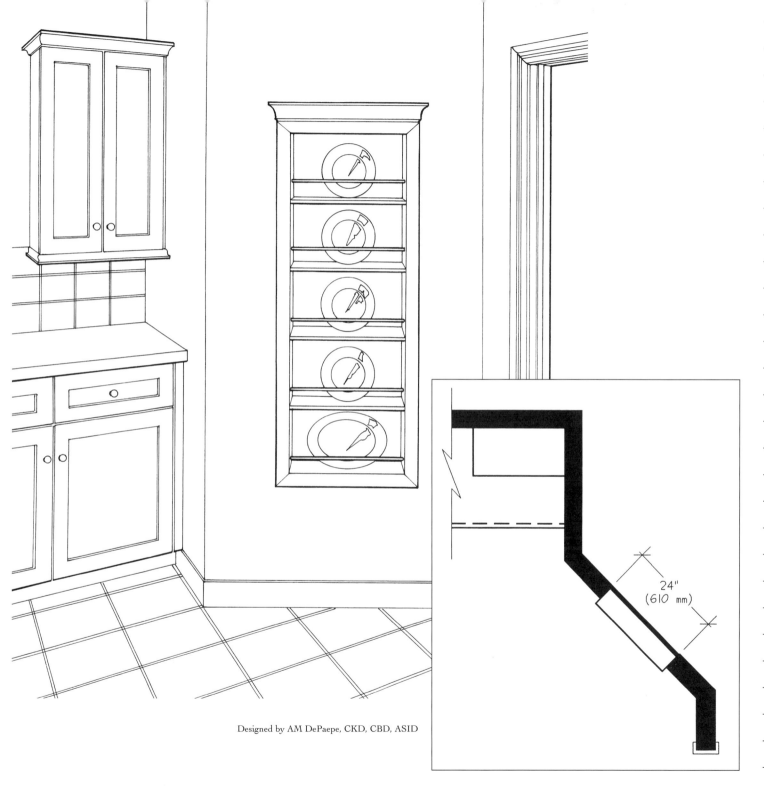

Designed by AM DePaepe, CKD, CBD, ASID

Got an awkward section of wall with no room for furniture or cabinets? Recessing shallow display shelves is a creative design solution. This 24"-wide x 60"-high Colonial-style cabinet displays plates or platters on 3"-deep shelves. The dishware is held in place with round rods that float 3" above each shelf. Additional Colonial details include simple clam shell casing and 3" cove molding.

24"
(610 mm)

Fretwork typically associated with a Victorian-era porch is brought inside to adorn this modern-day hutch. Swirls, stars and holes are cut out of the valance at the toe-kick and the sculpted back panel above the countertop. The base of the unit measures 48" wide x 24" deep and features three drawers above two doors. The wall-mounted portion of the hutch starts with a 48"-wide x 12"-deep open shelf. Below this shelf is a 24"-wide decorative shallow shelf unit with two detailed brackets. An 18"-wide x 12"-high pierced tin insert in the back panel peeks out from behind the shelves, contributing to the unit's unique look of layered fretwork.

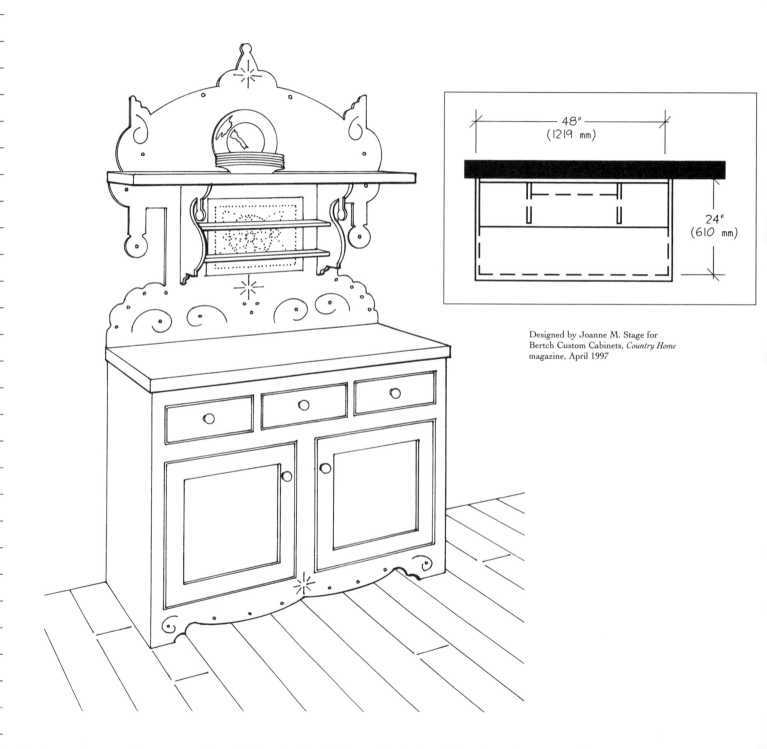

Designed by Joanne M. Stage for Bertch Custom Cabinets, *Country Home* magazine, April 1997

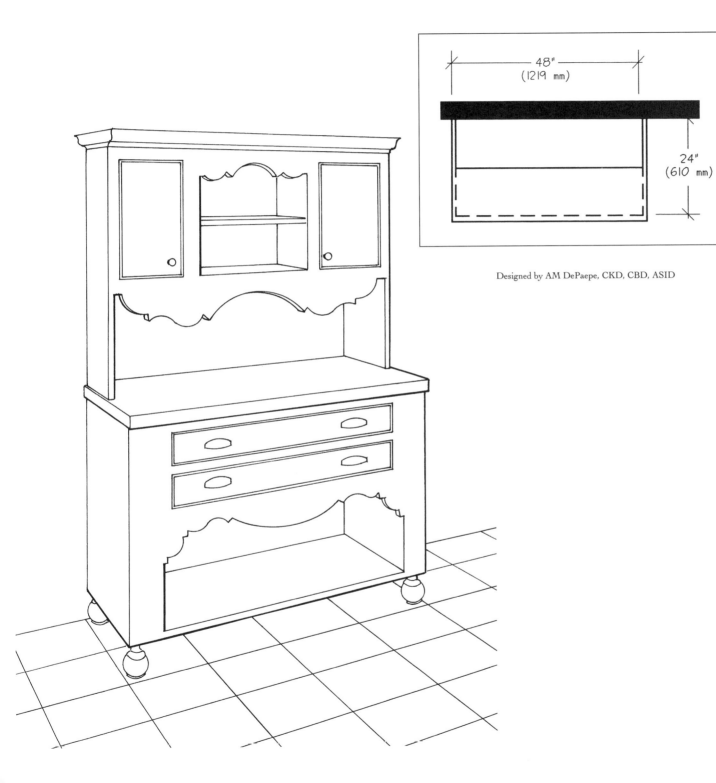

48"
(1219 mm)

24"
(610 mm)

Designed by AM DePaepe, CKD, CBD, ASID

Free flowing, curvilinear valances highlight the open display spaces of this freestanding hutch. Measuring 48" wide x 24" deep, the base is set atop four ball feet and features two 36"-wide drawers at the top and an open shelf at the bottom. Supported by extending its sides to the countertop, the hutch top includes two open shelves flanked by 12"-wide x 18"-high doors. Including the crown molding, the overall height of the unit is 75".

This display center is designed in conjunction with a cooking center. The bottom of the 36"-wide custom hood extends 6" beyond the hood's vertical face, creating a shelf to display either fine collectibles or culinary accessories. The 36"-wide professional-style cooktop below the hood is set above an additional display area. To accentuate the items on display, the open shelf base cabinet is adorned with a decorative arched valance with a cut out detail and keystone block molding.

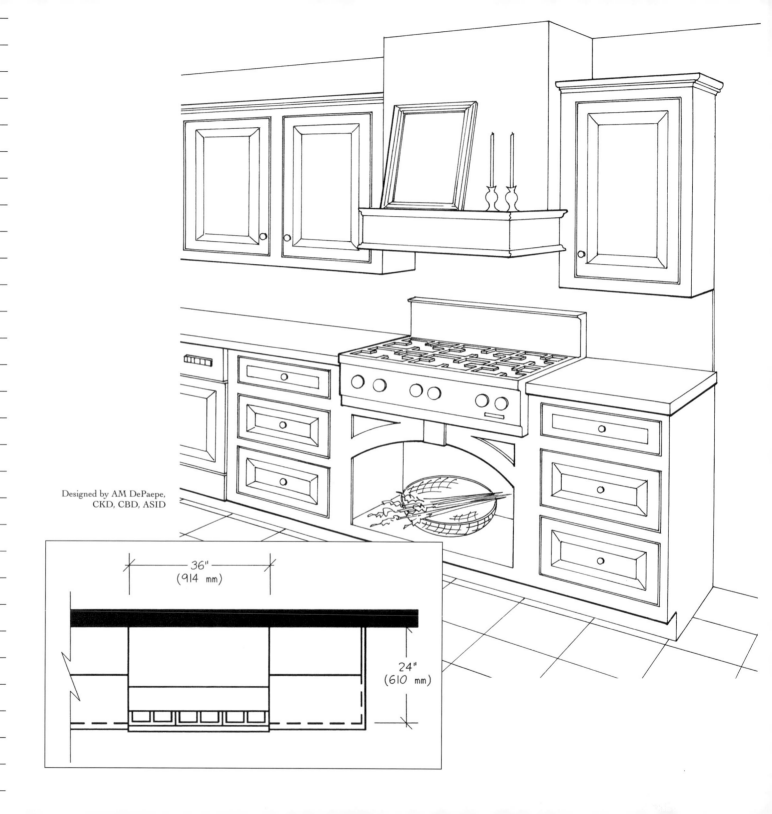

Designed by AM DePaepe,
CKD, CBD, ASID

36"
(914 mm)

24"
(610 mm)

CHAPTER SEVEN

Refrigeration Centers

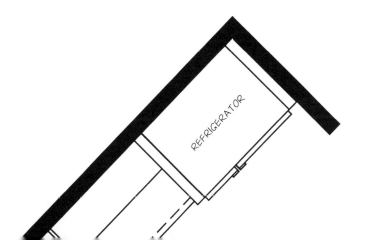

This storage center easily accommodates a freestanding refrigerator of standard depth and height. Ordering the tall enclosure cabinet 27" deep ensures maximum integration between the appliance and the surrounding cabinetry. Increasing the height of this cabinet from 84" to 90" contributes to the cohesive look, and allows room for a decorative display area. This area is adorned with an arched valance and beaded board paneling that matches the backsplash below. The wall and base cabinets to the left of the refrigerator are 36" wide, providing both storage and countertop landing space.

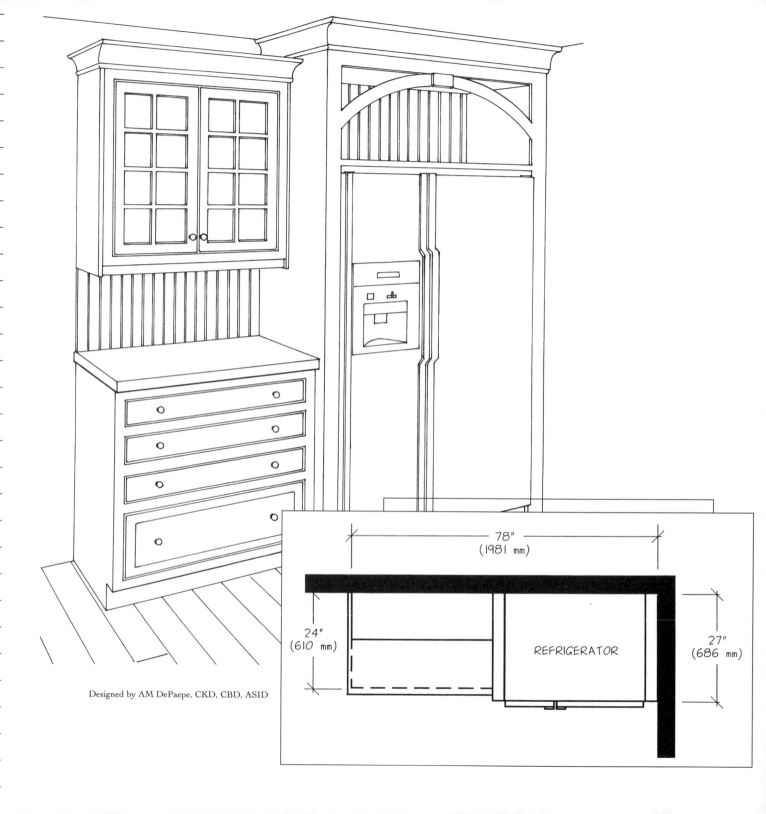

Designed by AM DePaepe, CKD, CBD, ASID

78"
(1981 mm)

24"
(610 mm)

REFRIGERATOR

27"
(686 mm)

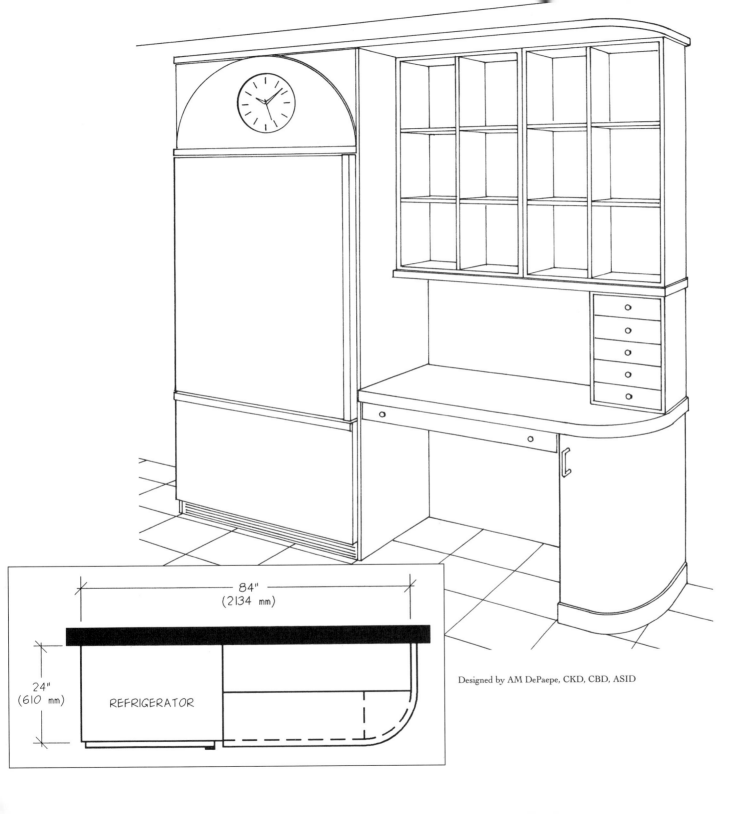

Designed by AM DePaepe, CKD, CBD, ASID

84"
(2134 mm)

24"
(610 mm)

REFRIGERATOR

Kids have no excuse for missing the school bus when a clock is built into the cabinetry above the refrigerator. This refrigerator measures 36" wide x 68" high x 24" deep and is enclosed by laminate panels that extend to 84" high. The clock is encased by two layers of panels above the refrigerator front. The first layer forms a 36"-wide x 16"-high rectangle that is closed at the top. The second layer is a 36"-diameter half circle with a 12"-diameter circle punctuating its center. The landing space next to the refrigerator doubles as a desk and continues the circular motif with a 12"-wide radius-base end cabinet. Twelve open storage cubes comprise the 48" x 48" wall storage. A 12"-wide column of five small drawers defines the boundary of the 36"-wide work surface.

Whimsical moldings and traditional paneling embellish a freestanding refrigerator, which makes up one center in this unfitted kitchen. The 36"-wide refrigerator is centered along a 39"-wide corner wall and attached to the return walls by two butterfly panels. Each panel measures 21" deep x 69" high and connects to the refrigerator with a 3"-wide angled filler. A heavy application of 9"-high moldings above the refrigerator and 4"-high furniture baseboard completes the unfitted style. Landing space is provided just 9" to the left of the side-by-side refrigerator by base cabinets that rest upon furniture legs.

Designed by Beth Stripling, CKD, CBD

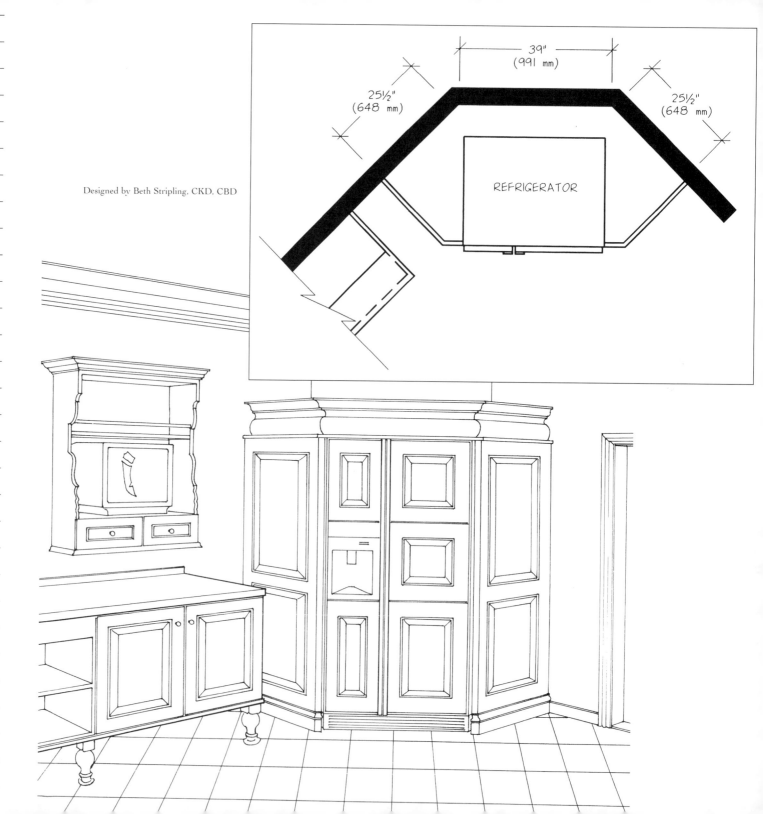

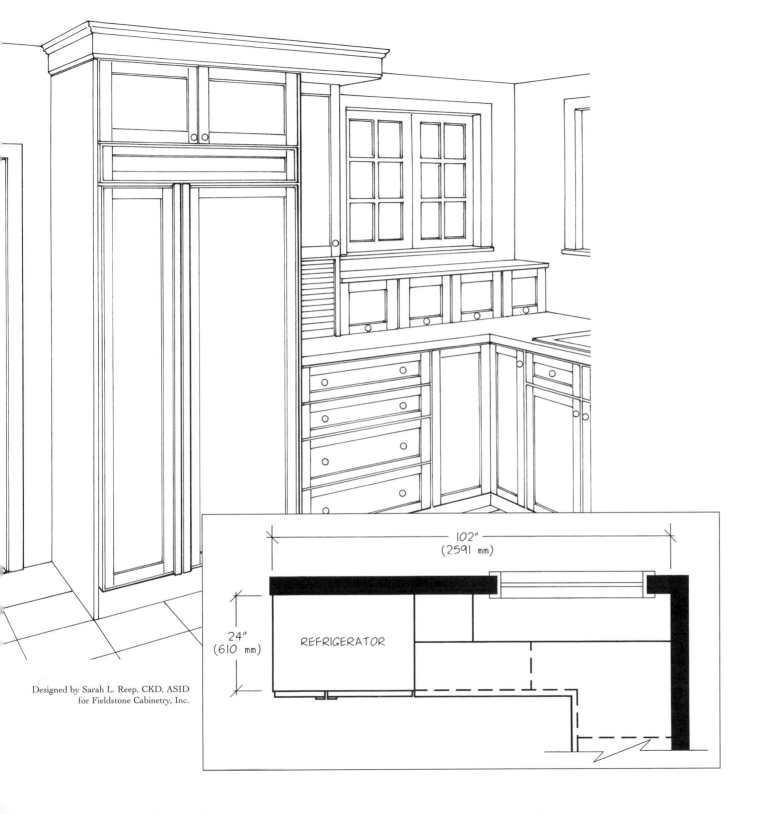

Designed by Sarah L. Reep, CKD, ASID
for Fieldstone Cabinetry, Inc.

102"
(2591 mm)

24"
(610 mm)

REFRIGERATOR

The 54" of countertop frontage provided between the refrigerator and sink in this design is designated as a sandwich making center to prepare school lunches. An 18"-wide wall tambour combination cabinet and four 12"-wide x 12"-high appliance garage units provide point-of-use storage and open to expand the counter area. The side-by-side, built-in refrigerator measures 36" wide x 84" high x 24" deep. It is enclosed by two side panels and a 36"-wide x 12"-high wall cabinet. A 30"-wide, four-drawer base and a 36"-wide lazy susan base round out the center's storage requirements.

When budget does not permit the purchase of a new built-in refrigerator, an existing refrigerator that measures 30" deep or more can be made to look like it is built in. Here, the illusion is accomplished by pulling the base lazy susan cabinet 12" from the left wall while extending the counter to the wall. Thus, an extra 36" of space is created to accommodate the deep refrigerator and a recessed tambour. A 36"-wide x 84"-high x 12"-deep pantry cabinet encloses the left side of the refrigerator and a 36"-wide wall cabinet is pulled out to 24" to close in the top. The result is not only more attractive than the typical installation method, but also increases access to storage and adds to the function of the work surface.

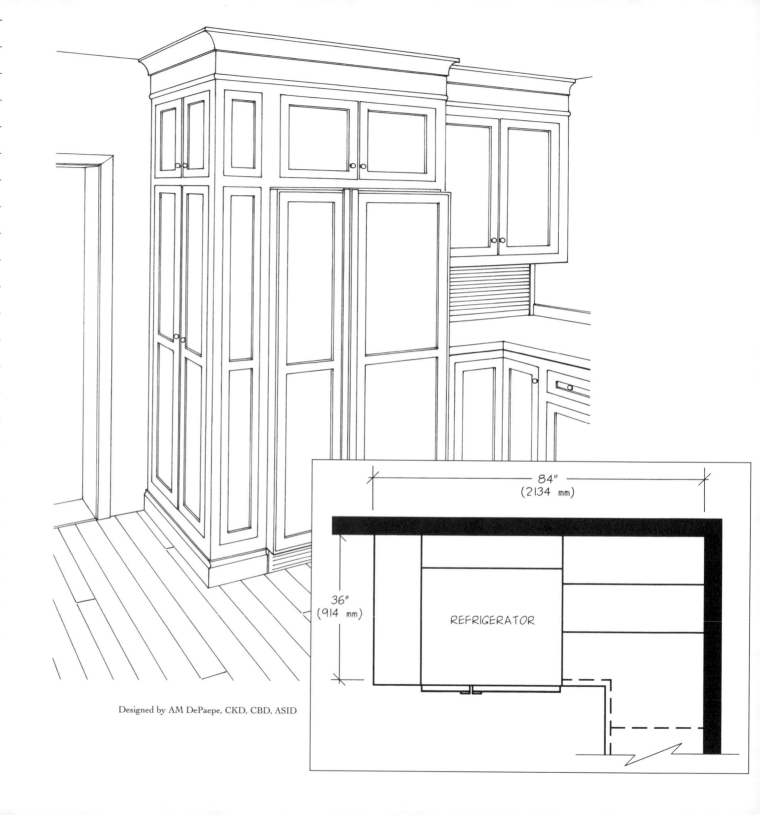

Designed by AM DePaepe, CKD, CBD, ASID

Designed by Nick Geragi, CKD, CBD, ASID

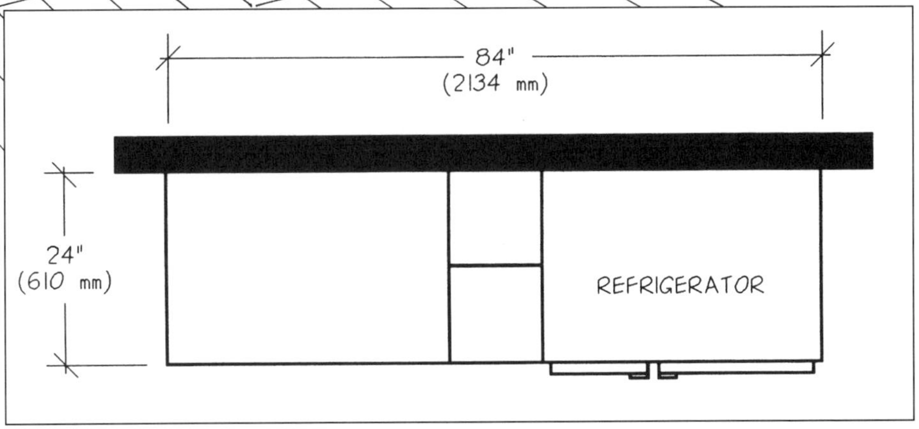

84"
(2134 mm)

24"
(610 mm)

REFRIGERATOR

Shaker-style simplicity and symmetry are the hallmarks of this freestanding refrigeration center. The design is accomplished by matching a tall pantry cabinet to the proportion of the refrigerator. The pantry's tall doors are aligned with those of the refrigerator. Repeating grilled glass-front doors across the elevation helps to make the center look like a cohesive unit. A 12"-wide open cabinet bisects this unit with a handy column of drawers and open shelves. These also align with the refrigerator doors.

This design makes a freestanding refrigerator part of the room's architectural detail. The refrigerator's 68" height and 30" depth is matched by 15"-wide custom cabinets on either side of the appliance. To maintain an uninterrupted line of cabinets and molding across the refrigeration center, 16"-high panels span the gap between the tall cabinets and the soffit. This follows the extra depth of the cabinets and forms an arched display niche above the refrigerator. A keystone molding, centered at the ceiling, highlights the entire design detail.

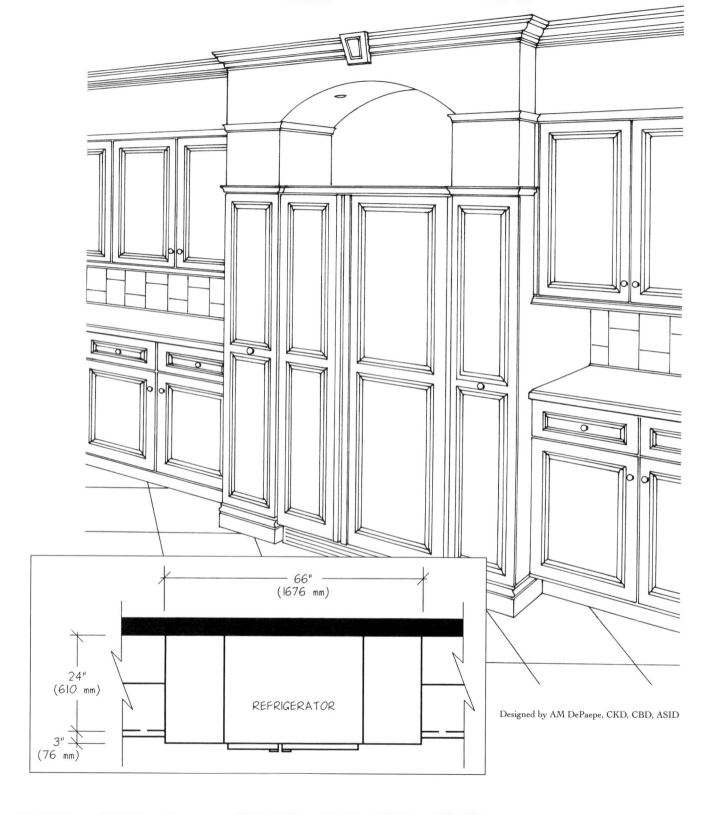

66"
(1676 mm)

24"
(610 mm)

REFRIGERATOR

3"
(76 mm)

Designed by AM DePaepe, CKD, CBD, ASID

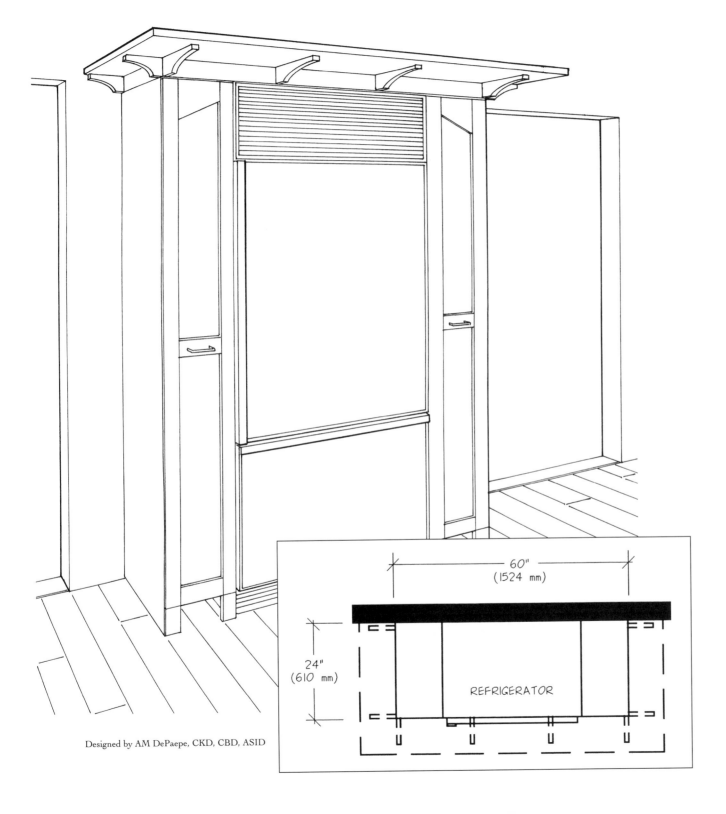

Designed by AM DePaepe, CKD, CBD, ASID

60"
(1524 mm)

24"
(610 mm)

REFRIGERATOR

The Arts & Crafts details of this refrigeration center make it look more like a piece of freestanding furniture. The center is comprised of a 36"-wide x 84"-high x 24"-deep refrigerator encased by two 12"-wide x 24"-deep pullout pantry cabinets. Arts & Crafts-style moldings around the top of the unit include eight wood brackets that support a 9" extended soffit board. **Design Note:** When landing space is not planned next to the refrigerator, NKBA Kitchen Planning Guidelines recommend providing counter space directly across the aisle from the appliance.

This refrigerator is set amid a grid of open storage cubes that make the contents easy to find and access by any member of the household. The refrigerator is 30" wide, 84" high and 24" deep. Two tall cabinets, each measuring 12"-wide, 90"-high and 24"-deep, flank the appliance, while a 30"-wide x 6"-high wine rack grid caps the top of the unit. All three pieces are tied together by 3/4"-wide, square-edged moldings repeated at the top of the flush toekick and above the cabinets. The open storage cubes have a false back; their exposed depth is 15".

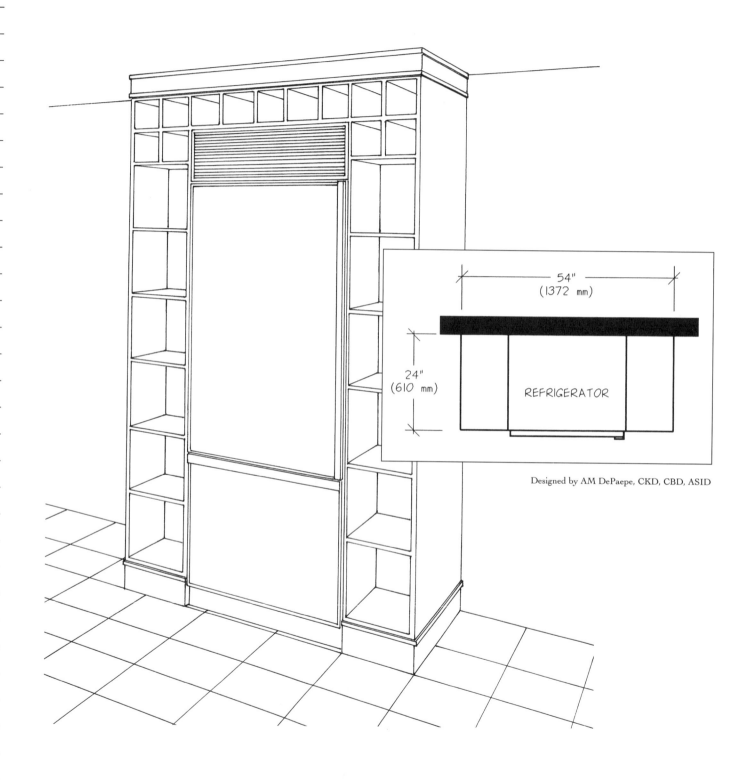

Designed by AM DePaepe, CKD, CBD, ASID

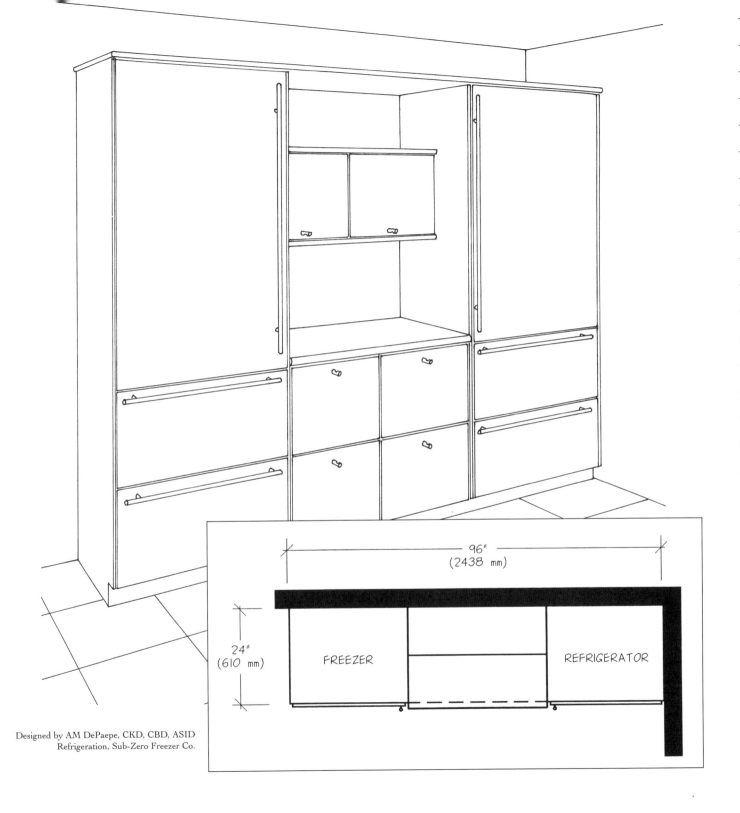

Designed by AM DePaepe, CKD, CBD, ASID
Refrigeration, Sub-Zero Freezer Co.

96"
(2438 mm)

24"
(610 mm)

FREEZER

REFRIGERATOR

This center takes advantage of the latest design advancements in refrigeration by offering total integration with standard cabinetry components. The two 30"-wide x 84"-high tall units on each end of the run of cabinets are the refrigeration appliances. The units are available as all-refrigerator, all-freezer or combination units. An undercounter drawer unit is also available. Shown here is an all-refrigerator unit on the right end and an all-freezer unit on the left. Between the appliances is 36" of storage and landing space.

Traditional-style cabinets frame two modern appliances in this refrigeration center. Starting at the left, the design features a 12"-wide x 24"-deep x 84"-high angled open shelf cabinet. Next is a built-in refrigerator that measures 36" wide x 24" deep x 73" high. This is topped by an 11"-high wall cabinet. Mirroring this setup is a built-in freezer with matching cabinetry. A 3"-high crown molding ties the four components together.

Design Note: Inserting a panel or blocking between the two appliances will improve the installation.

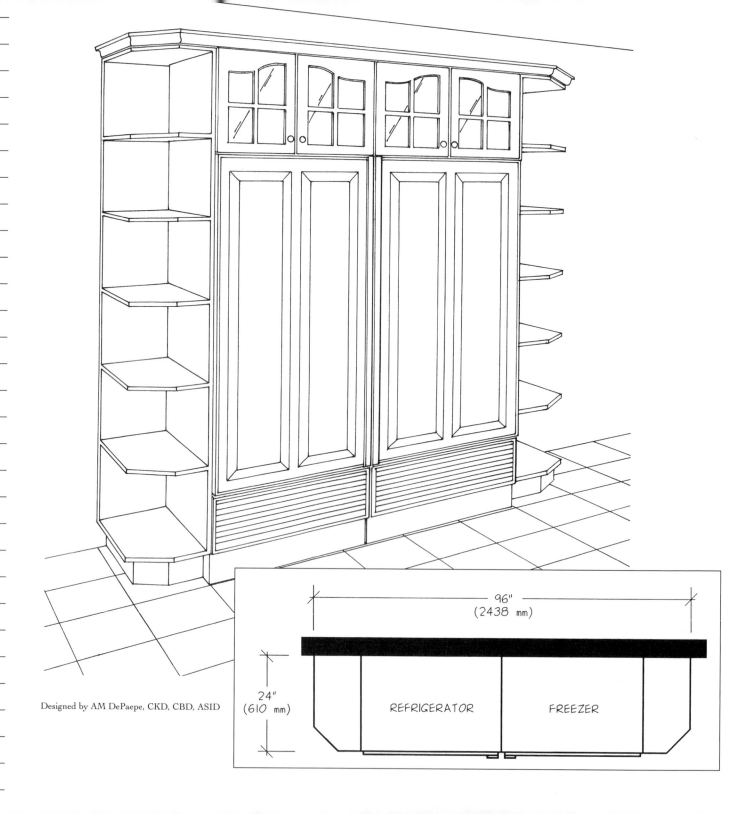

Designed by AM DePaepe, CKD, CBD, ASID

96"
(2438 mm)

24"
(610 mm)

REFRIGERATOR   FREEZER

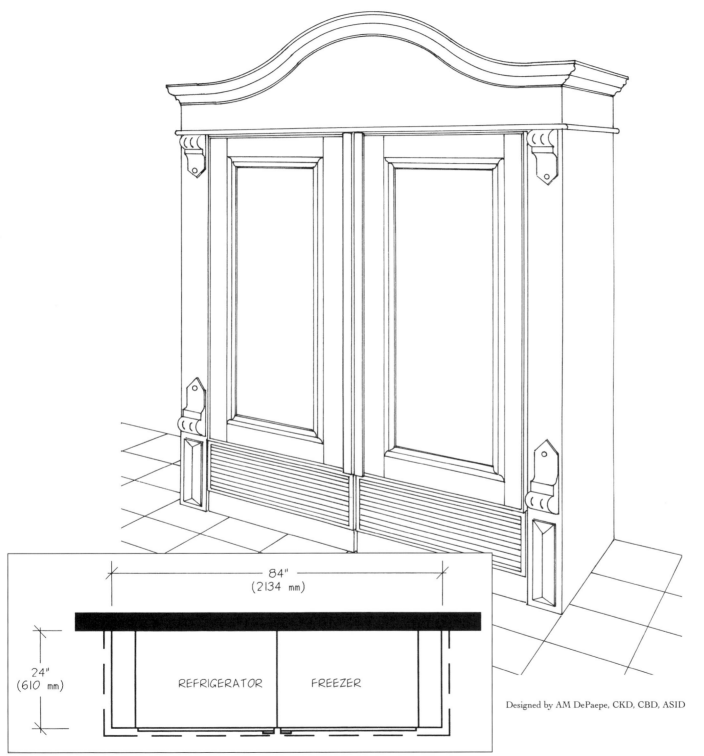

84"
(2134 mm)

24"
(610 mm)

REFRIGERATOR   FREEZER

Designed by AM DePaepe, CKD, CBD, ASID

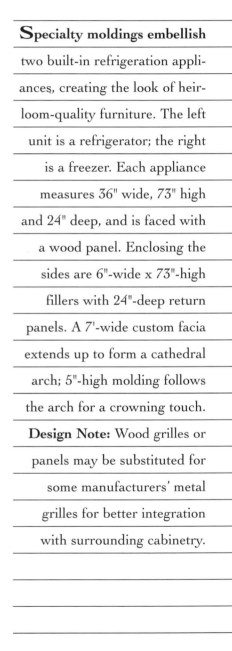

Specialty moldings embellish two built-in refrigeration appliances, creating the look of heirloom-quality furniture. The left unit is a refrigerator; the right is a freezer. Each appliance measures 36" wide, 73" high and 24" deep, and is faced with a wood panel. Enclosing the sides are 6"-wide x 73"-high fillers with 24"-deep return panels. A 7'-wide custom facia extends up to form a cathedral arch; 5"-high molding follows the arch for a crowning touch. **Design Note:** Wood grilles or panels may be substituted for some manufacturers' metal grilles for better integration with surrounding cabinetry.

Home Offices

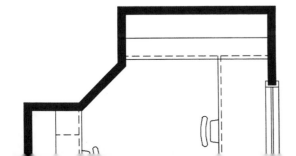

Introduction

By Patricia M. Swalander, CKD, CBD

With estimates of 30 to 43 million home offices at last count in 1996 — numbers that have been projected to grow — these spaces have become a profitable area of the home for kitchen and bath specialists.

The rise in the amount of people working from home, coupled with constantly changing technology, will make for increasingly sophisticated consumer demands. Issues such as electrical requirements, physical layout, separation of work areas from living space and entrance locations are presenting new challenges. Keeping up with the competition means considering several factors — many of which may be new to you — to make these rooms as safe, functional and fantastic-looking as the kitchens and baths you design.

Client Survey

Your client survey should include information about the type of business, the people who will use the office, and of course, their specific needs and requirements for equipment, storage and work space. Using the form on page 127 will help you make sure you're getting the information you need to design an office that's right for your client.

Functional Space

For the home office to be functional, it has to be designed for the specific activities of a client's business. Clearly, those who spend all day at a computer have different priorities than those who spend most of the day on the phone or meeting with clients. Architects and designers need room to spread out plans and samples. Accountants need a large desk space with easy access to their files and computer.

Organize work spaces according to major daily activities. For example, equipment used most often should be closest to the primary work center — in most cases the desk. Create as much surface area as possible to both serve as work space and accommodate the computer, phone, fax, copier and myriad other common office paraphernalia. Consider using pull-out or dropleaf tables to extend work surfaces.

U- and L-shaped layouts are most efficient for home offices. About 100 sq. ft. is enough to accommodate a U-shaped layout with a 36" to 48" space between the front and back work surfaces. Use an L-shaped layout for smaller spaces with two adjoining walls that are 5' to 6' each.

When space permits, create a sitting area for the homeowner to meet with a colleague or client without sitting behind a desk. This can be comfortably accommodated in 50 sq. ft.

When allocating space for office equipment, always consider electrical requirements, air circulation, noise and access for servicing. This is often a case of form following function. We might like to hide the technical tools of a business, but first it is crucial to keep them accessible.

Special Equipment

Ideally, the computer modem and fax should have dedicated phone lines. Adequate electrical capacity and separate phone lines are crucial to the smooth functioning of a home business. In newer communities, the number of phone lines is not usually a problem. In older or rural areas, you may be required to upgrade electrical and phone services. This may also be the ideal time to add a security system to the home.

Pay close attention to the requirements of any specialty equipment. Some electronic equipment requires a separate circuit. Remember to allow for amenities like a TV or coffee maker, and include the capacity for future expansion. Extra outlets ensure the copier will not have to be unplugged to vacuum the carpet. Surge protectors should be installed at the electrical panel or on individual outlets. Cable raceways built under the worktops will hold cable and cords and avoid a dangerous tangle of wires hanging down or laying across the floor.

Lighting and Air Quality

Office lighting must eliminate shadows and glare as well as illuminate work centers and provide general room lighting. A relatively simple way to provide flexibility is with dimmers, moveable fixtures and separate switching. Mount fixtures under upper cabinets and look for desk lamps that sit about 15" above the surface. Avoid placing fixtures where light will shine over the shoulder or directly down—especially over a computer. Window coverings should be designed to make use of natural light while controlling glare.

Since both machines and bodies generate heat and affect air quality, the office area should have separate heating and cooling controls. This will provide long-term benefits, since the busiest hours in the office and in the home generally do not coincide. Do not neglect good ventilation.

Office Ergonomics

Suiting the desk and chair to the individual's body stature will increase comfort and productivity while reducing the risk of repetitive strain injuries. Chairs should have adjustable backrests to support the lower back, with a seat that adjusts between 15" and 21" and inclines slightly forward to reduce pressure on the spine. The ideal chair has a stable base and is easy to get in and out of.

The computer keyboard should be adjustable and is best set at elbow level to keep the hands and wrists parallel to the floor. Keyboard trays are available with padded rests to support wrists. The best height is 1" to 2" below the desktop, which is typically 28" to 30" from the floor. The top of the monitor screen should be at eye level, about 20" away from the user. A common mistake is not allowing for sufficient knee space. Be sure to check for a comfortable clearance, including room to cross legs easily while sitting.

Storage

Storage is probably the most variable need in home offices. Some people keep everything on a few computer discs; others need a room full of filing cabinets. Some clients need to keep everything for years; others need only a few drawers. Be creative. On a practical note, avoid too much open shelving—it collects dust. Like in the kitchen, glass doors provide a similar feel that is easier to maintain. Pocket doors hide clutter while keeping necessities close at hand.

Patricia M. Swalander, CKD, CBD, has owned Heartwood Kitchen & Bath Design in Calgary, Alberta, Canada since 1980. She has served as president and national director of the NKBA's Prairie Provinces Chapter, and is the current secretary of the NKBA Board of Governors of Dealers. In addition to teaching kitchen and bath planning and renovation seminars and conducting presentations on home office design, Swalander is a frequent contributor to local and national publications.

Home Office Client Survey

Name of Client's Business _____

How much time does the client spend:

On the phone _____

On the computer _____

In meetings

with clients _____

with associates _____

Using job-specific equipment (list by type of equipment)

_____

_____

_____

General office duties _____

Other _____

What equipment does the client require?

Phone lines (fax/computer) _____

Job-specific equipment

_____

_____

_____

Electrical and mechanical requirements _____

Storage (type, quantity) _____

Furniture _____

Amenities (small refrigerator, coffee stations, powder room, etc.)

_____

_____

WHO will be using the home office?

How often? _____

Physical limitations _____

WHEN will the office be used? _____

_____

WHERE will the office be?

Separate from or integrated into the home? _____

Traffic patterns, privacy and noise constraints (include the needs of the primary user, the family and the clients)

_____

_____

_____

Do local bylaws exist for home offices? _____

_____

Future plans for the business and the home? _____

_____

_____

Budget? _____

_____

_____

The look? _____

_____

_____

This home office is designed for an interior designer and occupies about 125 sq. ft. It includes two separate work stations; one to the left of the window for a computer (see floor plan) and another to the right of the window for drafting. The storage and counter space underneath the window is designated for shared use by both work areas and serves as a counter for the telephone and fax machine. All counters are standard desk height, 30" above the floor, for maximim flexiblity. The opposite side of the room includes a tall bookcase for sample storage and a small sofa for impromptu meetings.

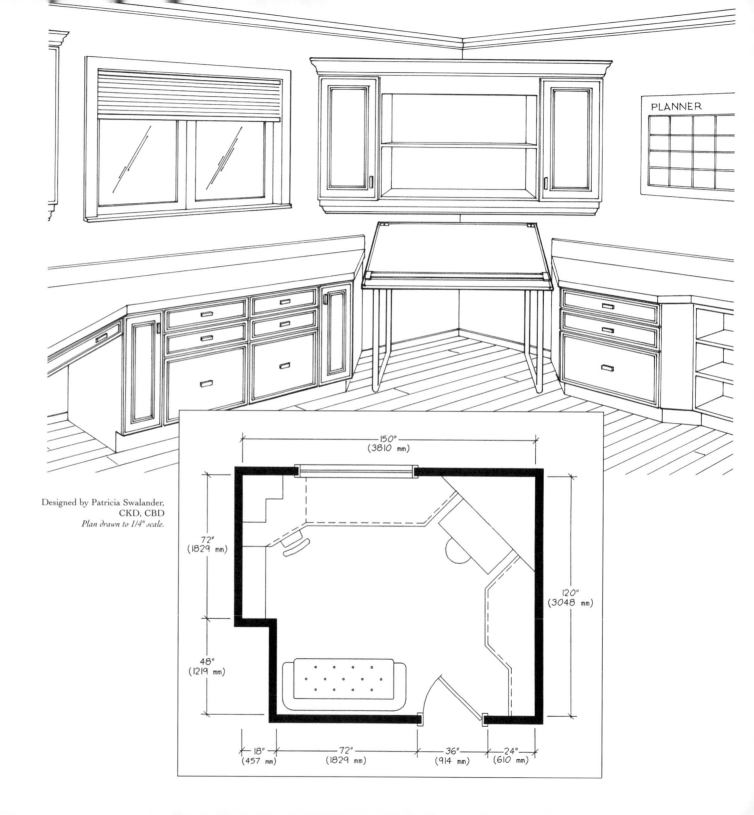

Designed by Patricia Swalander, CKD, CBD
Plan drawn to 1/4" scale.

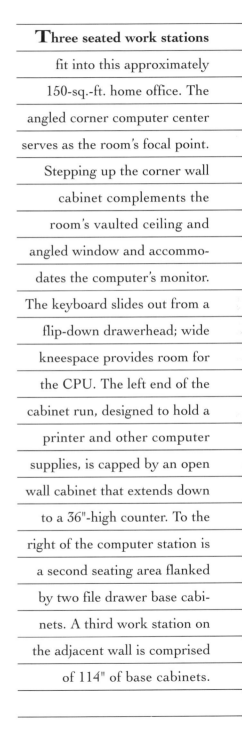

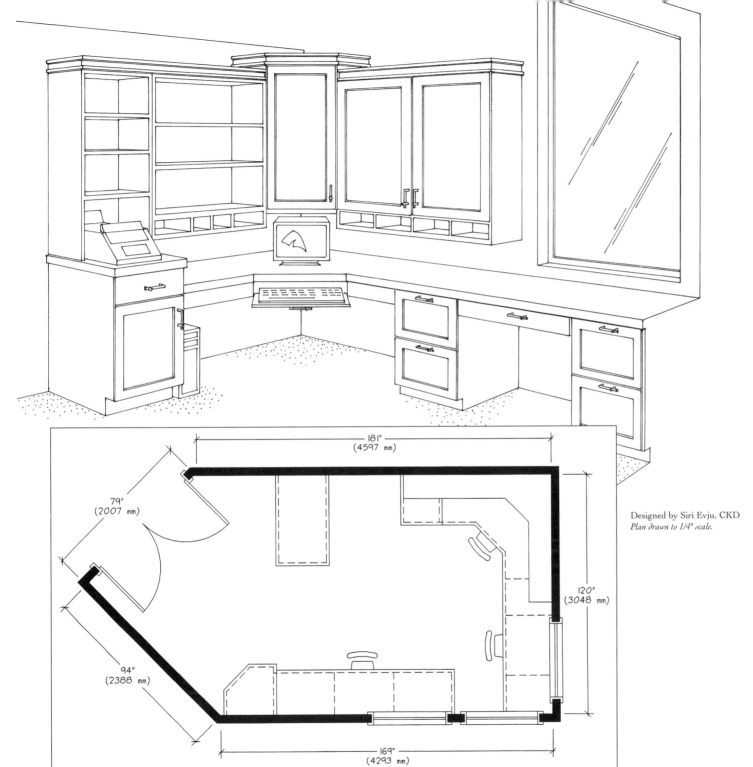

Designed by Siri Evju, CKD
Plan drawn to 1/4" scale.

Three seated work stations fit into this approximately 150-sq.-ft. home office. The angled corner computer center serves as the room's focal point. Stepping up the corner wall cabinet complements the room's vaulted ceiling and angled window and accommodates the computer's monitor. The keyboard slides out from a flip-down drawerhead; wide kneespace provides room for the CPU. The left end of the cabinet run, designed to hold a printer and other computer supplies, is capped by an open wall cabinet that extends down to a 36"-high counter. To the right of the computer station is a second seating area flanked by two file drawer base cabinets. A third work station on the adjacent wall is comprised of 114" of base cabinets.

Like a U-shaped kitchen, a U-shaped desk area maximizes efficiency. This one provides a smooth work surface transition from desk to double-sided work table that is perfect for working with a partner or meeting with a client. The work space starts at the left with a file drawer base. The remaining base area is dedicated to kneespace, making it easy for the user to spread out his or her work. A cork backsplash lines the wall directly above this area. Garage storage units—great for concealing equipment and papers when the office is not in use—line the wall below the windows. Open shelves provide additional accessible storage over the main desk and below the peninsula; 12"-deep tall storage fills the remaining wall space.

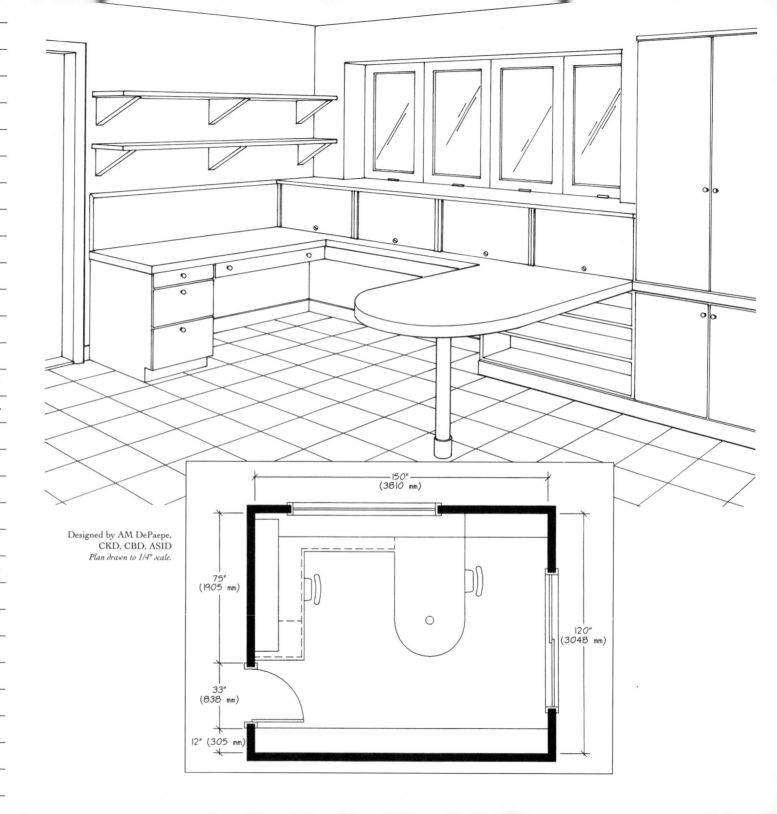

Designed by AM DePaepe,
CKD, CBD, ASID
Plan drawn to 1/4" scale.

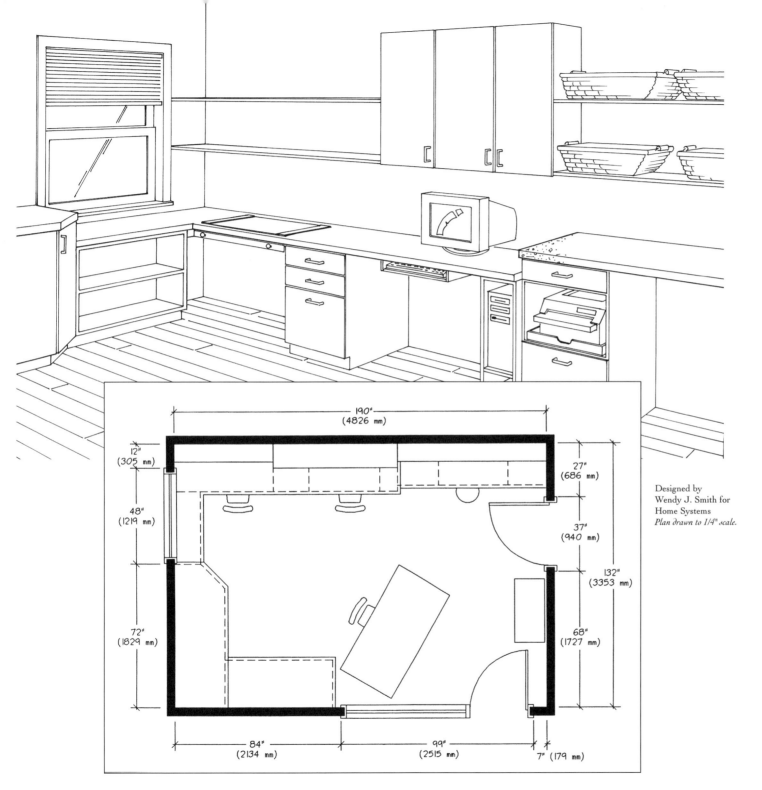

This home office was designed for a manufacturer's representative in the fashion industry. The desk was positioned to face the room's entrance and to take advantage of the outdoor view. Three additional seating areas accommodate other work-related needs: The corner station is for writing orders and accessing catalogues stored in the open shelves above. The space in the center holds the computer and incorporates an undercounter keyboard shelf and open base for the CPU. The third area is raised to stool height, providing a space for standing or seated users to look at fabric samples, which are stored in baskets on the shelves above. A freestanding copy machine fits neatly along the wall section between the two entries. The entire space is about 175 sq. ft.

Designed by
Wendy J. Smith for
Home Systems
Plan drawn to 1/4" scale.

190"
(4826 mm)

12"
(305 mm)

48"
(1219 mm)

72"
(1829 mm)

27"
(686 mm)

37"
(940 mm)

132"
(3353 mm)

68"
(1727 mm)

84"
(2134 mm)

99"
(2515 mm)

7" (179 mm)

This small 72-sq.-ft. home office is perfect for one person. The main work surface is 30" above the floor and approximately 6' wide. The counter surface extends into the windowsill, allowing the window to open right off the surface of the desk. Adjacent cabinetry utilizes 24"-deep x 36"-high standard kitchen base units and 48"-high wall cabinets that extend down to the counter with storage garages. The garages provide expanded counter space and allow the user to quickly hide messy or private papers. The room's opposite wall has a second seating area that accommodates a computer, printer and copy machine. A wood floor allows a single chair to easily roll from one work station to the other.

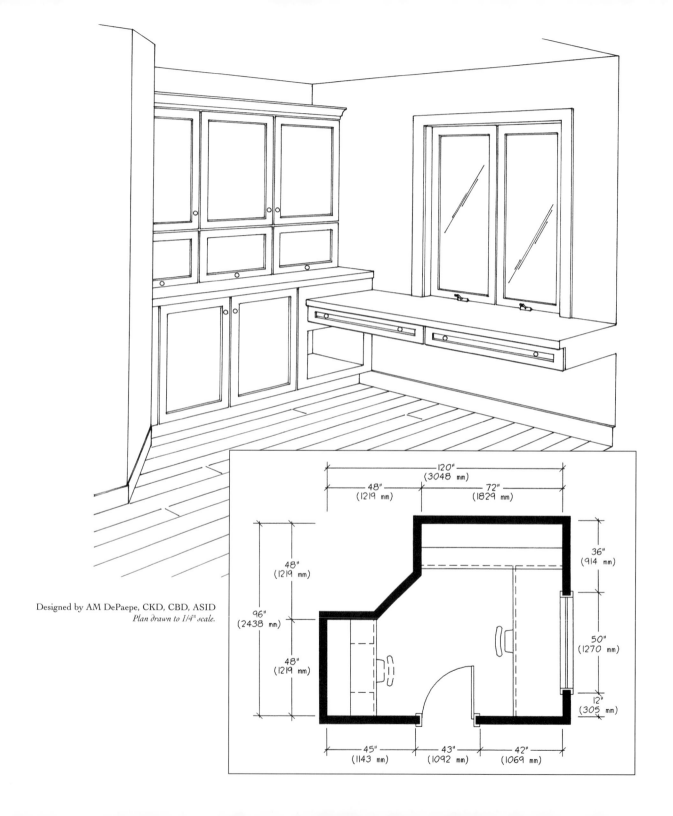

Designed by AM DePaepe, CKD, CBD, ASID
Plan drawn to 1/4" scale.

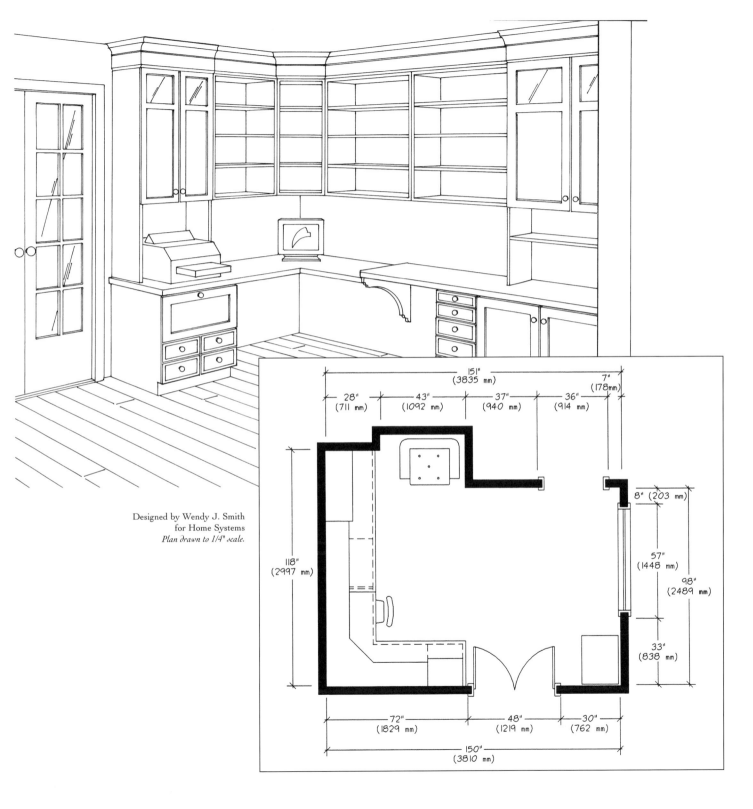

Designed by Wendy J. Smith
for Home Systems
Plan drawn to 1/4" scale.

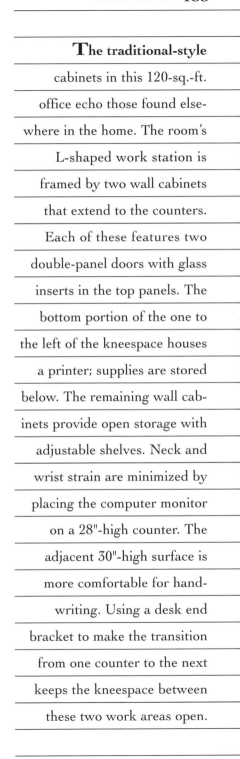

The traditional-style cabinets in this 120-sq.-ft. office echo those found elsewhere in the home. The room's L-shaped work station is framed by two wall cabinets that extend to the counters. Each of these features two double-panel doors with glass inserts in the top panels. The bottom portion of the one to the left of the kneespace houses a printer; supplies are stored below. The remaining wall cabinets provide open storage with adjustable shelves. Neck and wrist strain are minimized by placing the computer monitor on a 28"-high counter. The adjacent 30"-high surface is more comfortable for handwriting. Using a desk end bracket to make the transition from one counter to the next keeps the kneespace between these two work areas open.

A luxurious 307 sq. ft. provide a dramatic setting for this home office. Four entries allow access from inside and outside the home, plus an adjoining equipment room. A freestanding desk and seating area in the room's center maintains the traditional captain's seat arrangement (see plan). Behind the desk an arched countertop protrudes from the wall below a built-in marker-board cabinet. The opposite wall includes 17' of 30"-high counter. Base storage combines file drawers with full height doors. At the center of the run, an arched counter with 54" of kneespace below mirrors that on the opposite wall. This area is accented by fluted pilasters and corner block molding. The wall cabinets on either side extend to the counter with glass and solid doors.

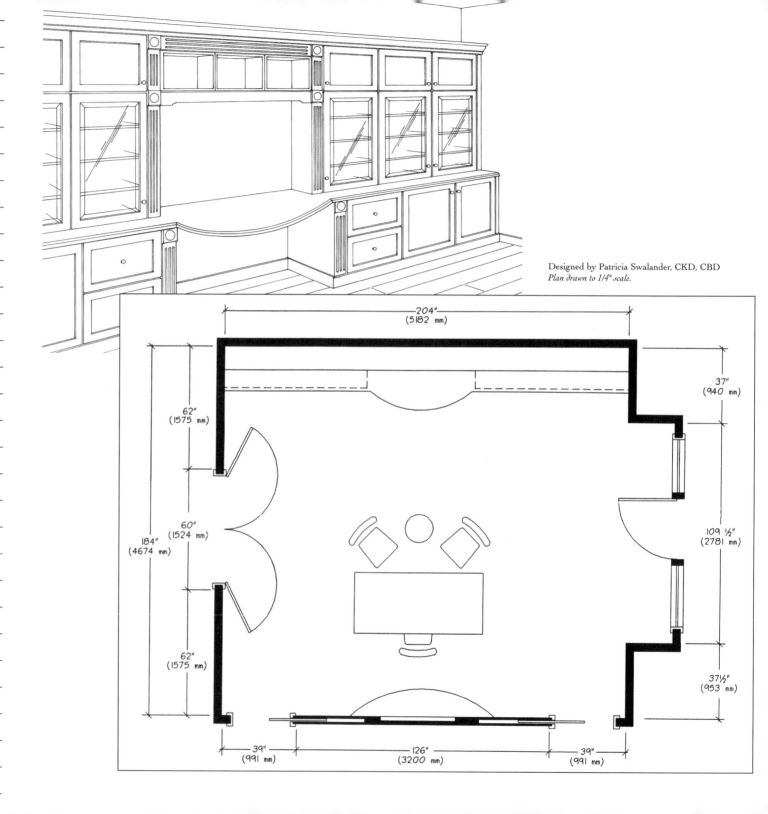

Designed by Patricia Swalander, CKD, CBD
Plan drawn to 1/4" scale.

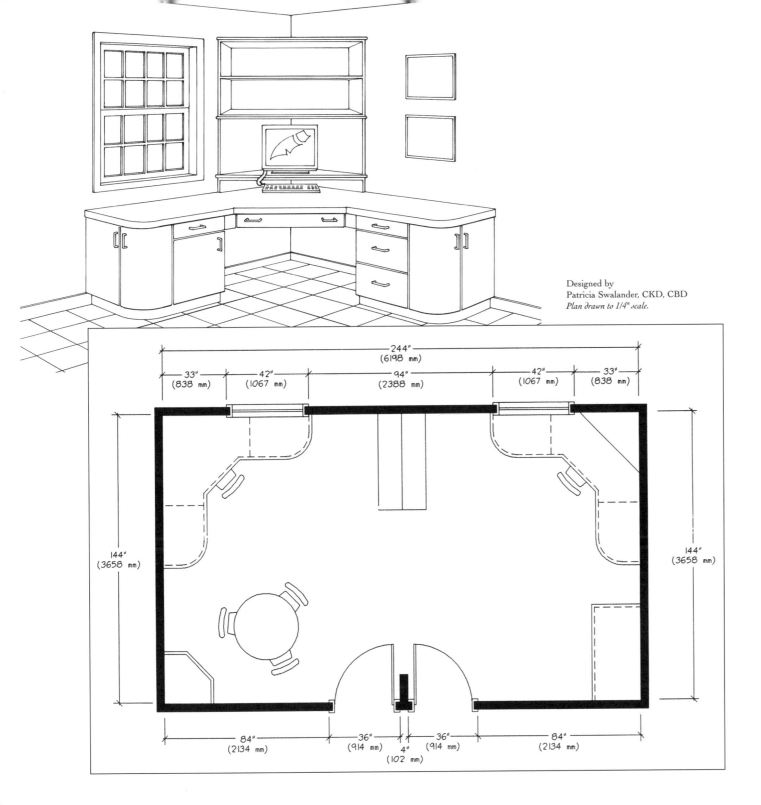

Designed by
Patricia Swalander, CKD, CBD
Plan drawn to 1/4" scale.

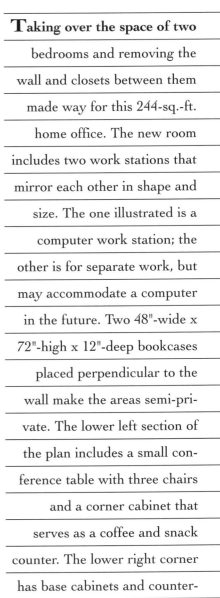

Taking over the space of two bedrooms and removing the wall and closets between them made way for this 244-sq.-ft. home office. The new room includes two work stations that mirror each other in shape and size. The one illustrated is a computer work station; the other is for separate work, but may accommodate a computer in the future. Two 48"-wide x 72"-high x 12"-deep bookcases placed perpendicular to the wall make the areas semi-private. The lower left section of the plan includes a small conference table with three chairs and a corner cabinet that serves as a coffee and snack counter. The lower right corner has base cabinets and counter-top space to hold a copier, fax machine and office supplies.

Adding a home office

does not always have to mean sacrificing a spare bedroom. This design accommodates the occasional guest by incorporating a fold-down bed and retaining the closet area. An L-shaped run of cabinets defines the office area; one leg measures 75", the other 132". Separate kneespaces serve separate functions: the first, located in the corner of the room, holds a computer with an open cabinet to the left for the CPU. The second is centered under a window to take advantage of the rural setting. At each end of the cabinet run open shelf wall cabinets are extended to the countertop; the left one features custom pigeon holes for paper storage. Cantilevering a soffit board over the window creates bonus storage space.

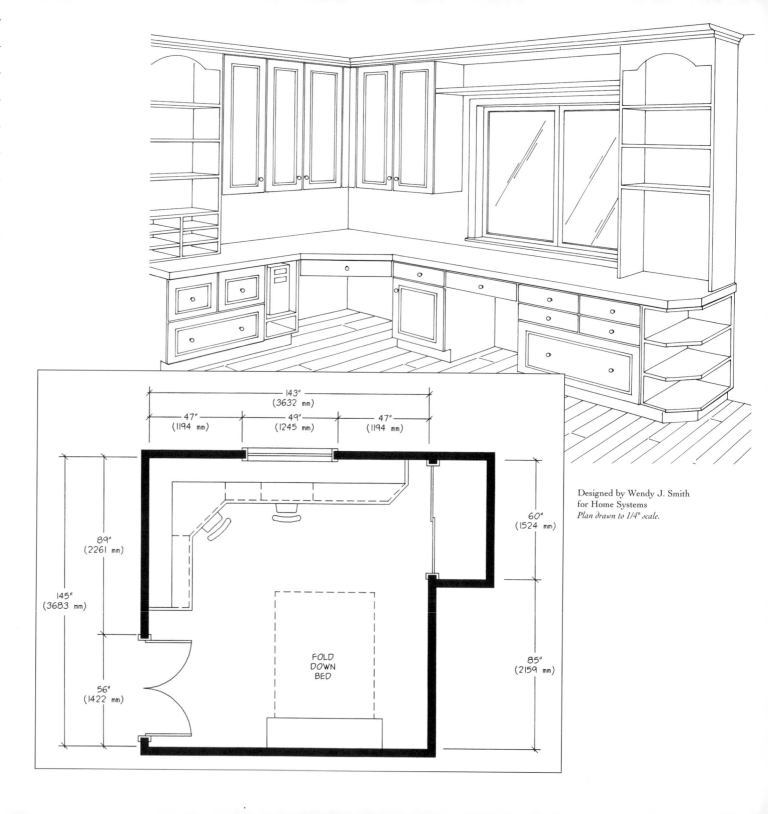

Designed by Wendy J. Smith
for Home Systems
Plan drawn to 1/4" scale.

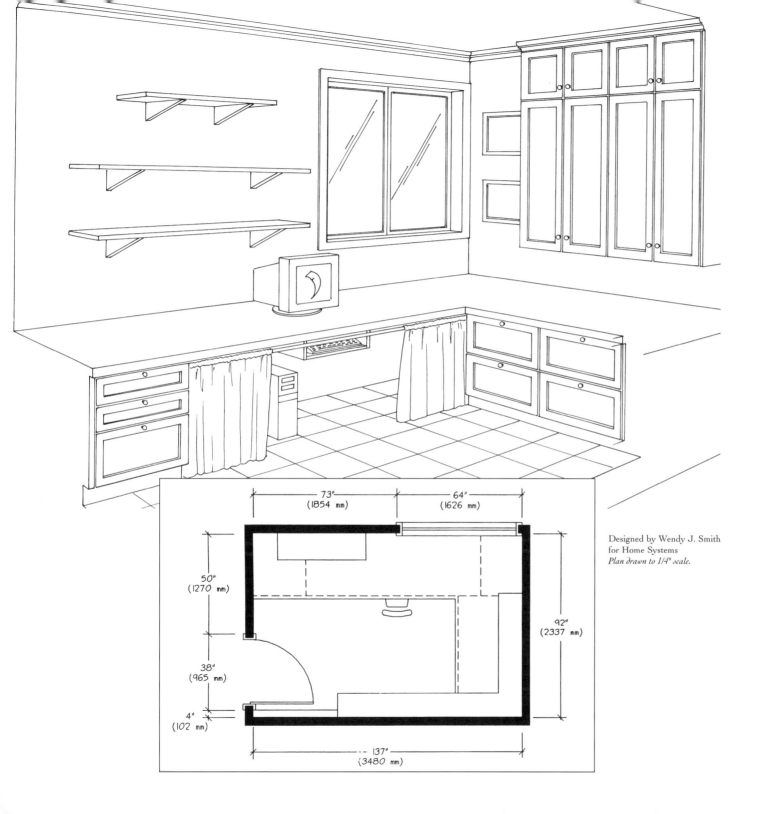

Designed by Wendy J. Smith
for Home Systems
Plan drawn to 1/4" scale.

Deep counters and hideaway storage for bins were the primary requests for this home-based developer's office. Installing 31"-deep counters met both requirements, allowing the user to spread out blueprints and finishing samples on the counter and providing open storage below for the bins. A fabric drape keeps the area neat. Base storage includes deep file drawers mounted on special-order slides. Wall storage combines open shelves to the left of the window with closed storage to the right. Tall, 12"-deep cabinets line the wall opposite the window and butt against adjacent wall cabinets. The 4"-deep area behind the door holds some of the home's utility controls behind a tall cabinet front. The door leads directly outside, providing privacy from rest of the home.

Contributing Designers

The author and *Kitchen & Bath Business* would like to extend a sincere thanks to the following designers and manufacturing companies who were gracious enough to share their kitchen center and home office designs:

Alan Asarnow, CKD, CBD, CR, Ridgewood, NJ

R. Kent Barnes, CKD, CBD, ASID, Austin, TX

Larry DeJong, CKD, Sioux Falls, SD

Kathleen Donohue, CKD, CBD, Portland, OR

Siri Evju, CKD, Beaverton, OR

Nick Geragi, CKD, CBD, ASID, Hackettstown, NJ

Wendy F. Johnson, CKD, CBD, Stamford, CT

Molly Korb, CKD, CBD, New Castle, CA

Mary Jo Peterson, CKD, CBD, Brookfield, CT

Plain & Fancy Custom Cabinetry, Shaefferstown, PA

Sarah L. Reep, ASID, CKD, Northwood, IA

Wendy J. Smith, Lafayette CA

Joanne M. Stage, CKD, CBD, New Canaan, CT

Beth Stripling, CKD, CBD, Fort Worth, TX

Scott Stultz, CKD, New Holland, PA

Patricia Swalander, CKD, CBD, Calgary, Alberta, Canada

Joan E. Zimmerman, CKD, CBD, Annapolis, MD

Sources

AGA Cookers
17 Towne Farm Ln.
Stowe, VT 05627
(800) 633-9200

Bertch Cabinet Manufacturing, Inc.
4747 Crestwood Drive,
Waterloo, IA 50702
(319) 296-2987

Country Home magazine
125 Park Ave.
New York, NY 10017-5529
(212) 557-6600

Fieldstone Cabinetry, Inc.
P.O. Box 109, Highway 105 East
Northwood, IA 50459
(515) 324-2114

GE Appliances
Appliance Park
Louisville, KY 40225
(800) 626-2000

Home Systems
The Forge, 3422 Mt. Diablo Blvd.
Lafayette, CA 94549
(510) 283-6638

Mepla, Inc.
909 W. Market Center Dr.
High Point, NC 27261-1469
(910) 883-7121

National Kitchen & Bath Assoc.
687 Willow Grove St.
Hackettstown, NJ 07840
(800) THE-NKBA

Outwater Plastics Industries, Inc.
4 Passaic St.
Wood Ridge, NJ 07075
(800) 631-8375

Plain & Fancy Custom Cabinetry
P.O. Box 519, Rte. 501 and Oak St.
Schaefferstown, PA 17088
(717) 949-6571 for your nearest rep
Note: Plain & Fancy is only distributed east
of the Mississippi

Raymond Enkeboll Designs Co.
16506 Avalon Blvd.
Carson, CA 90746-1096
(310) 532-1400

StarMark Cabinetry
600 East 48th St. North
Sioux Falls, SD 57104
(800) 755-7789

Sub-Zero Freezer Company, Inc.
P.O. Box 44130
Madison, WI 53744-4130
(800) 222-7820

The YesterTec Design Company
P.O. Box 190
Center Valley, PA 18034
(610) 838-1194

Work Smarter –Not Harder!

Competition has never been fiercer. Don't fall behind! These great books from Kitchen & Bath Business help you design, sell and run your business better.

NEW! How to Design Creative Kitchens and Baths

by Morton Block, CKD, CBD, IIDA. $39.95

Develop dynamite designs that sell! Learn the touches that turn a layout from sufficient to sensational. Whether you're a beginner or an experienced pro, this book has valuable information to help you sharpen your skills and wow your clients. 160 pages.

NEW! How To Start and Run a Successful Kitchen and Bath Business

by Morton Block, CKD, CBD, IIDA. $39.95

Here's how to run a leaner, meaner and cleaner operation. Develop a successful business plan; choose a prime location; evaluate your target customer; deal with contracts, design fees and retainers; and track financial progress. A bonus resource guide puts important contacts at your fingertips. Tired of putting out fires all day? Planning to take the plunge and start a new business? This is the book you MUST have. 128 pages

100 Plus Great Ideas for Moldings

by Annette DePaepe, CKD, CBD, ASID. $39.95

Moldings are the hottest design accents around for kitchen and bath designs. They easily make a narrow room appear wider or bring a too-high ceiling down to a manageable scale. Give your designs a unique look and feel by combining molding materials, designs and patterns. Here are over 100 creative ideas with detailed work drawings, arranged in easy-to-access fashion by location and purpose. 166 pages.

100 Great Ideas for Islands

by Annette DePaepe, CKD, CBD, ASID. $39.95

Islands serve as dramatic focal points in any kitchen design. In this comprehensive book you'll find 100 of the freshest designs for islands, all with work drawings and dimensions, divided by architectural elements or styles. A bonus chapter shows practical kitchen planning desks and message centers. 142 pages.

NEW!
Dangerous Clients: How to Protect Yourself
by Susan Edwards Ph. D. $39.95

Is that new client likely to sue you? Are you going to be called to the job site every day just to hold Nervous Nellie's hand? Does she want a new kitchen, or does she want to play mind games? The custom nature of your business demands that you know the psyche of the homeowner and recognize troubles before they happen. This book tells you how. 160 pages

How To Be A Better Manager
by Hank Darlington. $29.95

Unless you're a one-man band, it's a good bet that most of your time as an owner/manager is spent on "people" problems. Here, KBB's acclaimed columnist dispenses practical advice on hiring, managing, motivating and terminating employees, as well as on handling issues before they become problems. An appendix features human resource forms you can adapt. 90 pages.

How To Be A Smart Marketer
by Mercedes B. Aza. $29.95

You may not be a home center chain with a fat marketing budget, but you can still get your products and services to sell themselves to your clients. Here are specific steps you can take to define your target market and make sure it gets your message, through advertising and word of mouth. 118 pages.

NEW!
100 Great Ideas for Kitchen Centers
by Annette M. DePaepe, CKD, CBD, ASID. $39.95

Design creative cooking centers, cleanup centers, food preparation centers, laundry centers and more. KBB's 100 Great Ideas for Kitchen Centers showcases inspirational floor plans and perspectives for the job-specific centers that are essential to today's kitchens and baths. Plus, a bonus chapter on home office design features 10 floor plans with perspective drawings and a special client survey. 142 pages